NECESSARY CANDOR

Standing Up To Racial Discrimination and Bullying In the Workplace

AND SURVIVING THE ONSLAUGHT IMPOSED FOR COMPLAINING

John D. Bumphus, Jr.

John D. Bumphus, Jr.

DanBump Publishing Group products are available at special quantity discounts for bulk purchase for sales promotions, premiums, and educational needs. For details, write DanBump Publishing Group, 221 South Myrtle, Edwardsville, Illinois 62025.

For Speaking Engagements for Mr. John D. Bumphus, contact Joda Management at (480) 232-3350.

Standing Up to Racial Discrimination and Bullying In the Workplace
by John D. Bumphus, Jr.
DanBump Publishing Group
221 South Myrtle
Edwardsville, Illinois 62025
Email us at: danbumppublishing@gmail.com
Visit the website at www.danbumppublishing.com

ISBN-10: #1495927784

Printed in the United States of America

NECESSARY CANDOR

By

John D. Bumphus, Jr.

Table of Contents

Standing Up To Racial Discrimination and Bullying In the Workplace

AND SURVIVING THE ONSLAUGHT IMPOSED FOR COMPLAINING

Introduction

Every work day, literally millions of black people in America feel as if they are being racially marginalized, disregarded or disenfranchised while on the job and at work by their white employers and co-workers. The general and socially accepted option of action for these black people is to learn to "go along to get along"; that is, to "keep working on your job", unless things happen to just get too crazy. "Too crazy", you ask? Yes, each and every black American has, and always holds onto, their own individual perception, idea and understanding about how much, is too much, for any person to be asked to put up with, just in order to "keep your job".

Of course and rightly, filing an in-house complaint of racial discrimination is the most expedient and accepted form of resolving any issues which may come into dispute. Most companies are adequately equipped with Human Resource Departments designed to observe and monitor these occurrences, so as to effectively adapt, and change their policies and practices when necessary, in a timely enough manner to avoid the costly legal expenses of outside litigation. When an in-house complaint has been filed, with no resolution appearing to be forthcoming, the next general option is to take that complaint to the Equal Employment Opportunity Commission, or EEOC. Also, and in the event where the worker is a union member in good standing, oftentimes the assigned union shop steward will correctly intervene, address and bring the complaint personally to company management, in lieu of having to involve the EEOC. And then ultimately, if that dues-paying union member finds no resolution from filing a legitimate complaint with the company, in addition to receiving no assistance from the union which steadfastly receives his oftentimes mandatory dues payments, the last sensible optional first step is a visit to the overseeing entity of all America's unions, the National Labor Relations Board, or NLRB.

Unfortunately, and far too frequently, not everyone presented with workplace issues of pent-up rage based upon racial discrimination seeks the socially accepted bureaucratic path to resolution; the matter can then tragically turn to de-evolve into situational workplace violence. For these people, who have willfully chosen the path of self-destructive violence, instead of seeking the practical remedy of procedural justice, along with the intervention of psychological counseling, as a remedial measure, they never find that they could have found a potentially life-saving medical option; sadly however, very many people continue to view the social stigma associated with seeing a psychologist as a personal failing of appearing to be weak, or personally not being unable to cope with pressure, while implicitly not understanding that asking for help when you realize you need it, IS the best form of coping.

The Canons of Legal Ethics require that an accused defendant employer must receive a zealous defense representation. This is a very basic legal tenet which actually establishes the base, and then in turn, the profit margin, for the overall industry of employment law. In the business world, most corporations choose to designate and retain an attorney as the official legal representative member of their administrative staff. These attorneys, whom are also known as General Counsel or corporate counsel, are usually assigned to serve as the gatekeepers for potential ethical dilemmas. It is thereby generally perceived to be the duty of these in-house legal counsel to anticipate, observe, and quash unethical decisions and business practices, long before any developing complaints can even grow in stature enough to reach corporate supervisory, or administrative, personnel for consideration. However, in an event where and when the corporate General Counsel actually becomes the bad actor in an ethical drama, the stage becomes set for what can appear, and feel to be, as if the very doors of a mythic and dangerous underworld have been opened for full review.

The deliberate serious and willful causation, and manipulative, bad-faith handling of, my California Workers' Compensation claim of a psychological stress injury caused by racial discrimination against the California company known as the TIMEC Company, Inc., which is an oil refinery industrial maintenance contractor based in Vallejo CA, shall be revealed and exposed here in its most blatant and unseemly chronological glory. I believe it to be essential that every corporation and employer who chooses or intends to operate against any of their employees in the manner chosen by the TIMEC Company in their demonstrative stance against my interests as a human being, should be forewarned on the public record of opinion, that the actual concept of "being made whole" as a legal consequence may very well include a writing of this sort being created and published. By way of their overt refusal to comply with the very simple and basic rules of employment law, the TIMEC Company of Vallejo, CA, displayed a wholly unethical and intentionally illegal, racially bigoted pattern of actions in their legal dealings with me. I have chosen this current time as one ripe, and right, for me to finally begin sharing this memoir about the totally unexpected and non-anticipated, horrific pro se experiences in employment law litigation I encountered with their organization as my legal adversarial entity.

It seems very odd to me that all of the so-called "gains" in racial relations are publicly measured by the successes black people have courageously managed to obtain after living through being a rigidly and collectively suppressed people, while no focus at all seems to be placed upon keeping track and measure of the constant and enduring tidal flow of racist discontent and malevolent social actions on the part and in behalf of bigoted white people. White people have politically, socially and corporately misbehaved with impunity and with an expanding, seemingly measured, sense of gradual immunity, via various and onerous "Jim Crow" law legislation, ever since the so-called end of slavery. The common sociological perception of "Growth in America", while allowing for a few talented and gifted black people to emerge socially and financially, has yet systematically continued to serve to disenfranchise the entire mass of poor people of color.

And against those poor people of color, the White Privilege Index is consistently utilized to ensure, in South African Apartheid fashion, that any so-called "rules" or "laws" can be twisted, and/or ignored if, and whenever deemed as necessary, in order to maintain the prominence of the white American status quo. "Reverse Discrimination" against white people is the courtroom legal rationalization which quickly and immediately poked holes in American Affirmative Action policies, before those new laws even got a chance to get started, while the sole, current black United Supreme Court Justice, also sometimes known, and referred to, as Clarence "I Got Mine" Thomas, who is, by far, the most prolific beneficiary of Affirmative Action in all of American history, steadfastly rallies against the enforcement of this sociological adjustment principle of the so-called "race quotas" system, when and wherever the topic comes up.

The reality of the evolution of my injury is that the President of TIMEC Company, Inc., Gary French, and TIMEC's administrative corporate lawyer, General Counsel Brent Babow, initially set the stage for its occurrence on December 3, 1993, by putting on a show of pretending to be sincere about teaching an employee relations class entitled, "Legal Issues for Supervisors". I was then subsequently initially injured by the Serious and Willful Misconduct of TIMEC-Shell Martinez CA Superintendent Geno Kitsch's hostile work environment unmitigated hubris in actually twice attempting to intimidate me; once semi-privately, and then on another time, publicly before the entire TIMEC-Shell workforce, into submissive silence about my sincere desire to complain about an overt instance of racial discrimination, an incident which had already recently delivered a direct and instant negative financial impact upon me.

I was subsequently illegally terminated from employment with the TIMEC Corporation on January 19, 1995 due to an unlawful discharge based upon my complaining about racial discrimination. The irony of the situation is that it was a SECRET and unlawful TIMEC administrative termination, one totally unbeknownst to me, which in turn served as the "set-up" for their post-employment campaign to destroy me, by assault through illicit and punitive litigation techniques, of which I was initially totally unaware.

My injury was further complicated and exacerbated as it became a cumulative stress injury, inspired by the horrific action of TIMEC Company Director of Human Resources, Barry Raymos' perfunctory ruse of pretending to interview me pertaining to the investigation of my written complaint of racial discrimination, while all the while knowing that he had already taken it upon himself to shred my complaint and any notes he may have had pertaining to the existence of the matter. All of this insidious information pertaining to my injury was always available and accessible for TIMEC's Workers' Compensation Risk Management Claims Administrator Sue Evans who, according to the State of California Permissibly Self-Insured (PSI) agreement in place at that time, was required by law to utilize every bit of that same vital information and knowledge to protect me, as an injured TIMEC employee.

This memoir, which has been villainously imposed upon my conscious and subconscious mind by the TIMEC Company, Inc., is now being publicly set forth so as to be available for all, in the hope and prayer that everyone else psychologically stressed and assaulted, by any form of bigotry in their workplace, may choose to seek and receive justice. As I guide you through the Necessary Candor involved in traveling my emotional journey towards achieving peace of mind, I also desire that everyone reading this realize the importance of seeking the help of professional counseling, along with utilizing strength from their God within, in order to find and implement non-violent ways to expose the wrongdoings of racist employment practices to the world. I also commit to continue sharing my subjective perspectives on workplace racism and its ongoing societal detriment, because I intend that the reality of this actual expression of my publicly calling out the TIMEC Company Inc., due to their chosen actions, and their inactions pertaining to this important issue of racial discrimination, shall somehow take permanent hold as an actual component to their workplace racial relations policies and practices. Therefore, this dialogue is my parting gift, to them.

Prologue

I was born in 1954, the year the United States Supreme Court ruled on the landmark school desegregation case entitled *Brown vs. Board of Education*, 347 U.S. 483, in which the Court declared state laws establishing separate public schools for black and white students to be unconstitutional.

My African-American second grade teacher at the racially integrated Highland Elementary School of Vallejo, CA, Mrs. Dorothy Jean Fitzgerald Brown, was an elder cousin to Linda Brown of the *Brown* case, and had previously been named as the plaintiff in prior desegregation litigation in their Topeka, Kansas community; litigation which served as background impetus to the landmark Supreme Court case.

In the 1963 summer between my third and fourth grade years, United States President John F. Kennedy gave the first nationally televised speech by a white man arguing for justice and relief concerning the racist oppression of black people in America; hours later, black civil rights activist Medgar Evers was assassinated with a shot in the back by white racist Byron De La Beckwith.

In August of that same 1963 summer, over three hundred thousand people peacefully held a racially integrated and socially diverse march on Washington D.C., while rallying for civil and economic rights; two weeks later, the 16th Street Baptist Church in Birmingham, Alabama was bombed on Sunday morning by white racists Robert "Dynamite Bob" Chambliss, Bobby Frank Cherry and two others, killing four young black girls, and injuring 22 other people.

During my fourth grade year at the Highland School, on November 22, 1963, that same white United States President John F. Kennedy, who in June of that year gave the nationally televised speech arguing for justice and relief concerning the racist oppression of black people in America was murdered, just like Medgar Evers was, with a rifle shot from behind, before the nation, and before the whole world, while waving to the citizens of Dallas, Texas, from the back of the Presidential Limousine.

In the summer between my fourth and fifth grade years at the Highland School, United States President Lyndon Baines Johnson signed the Civil Rights Act of 1964. This Act served to legally outlaw major forms of discrimination against racial, ethnic, national and religious minorities, and also women. Title VII of that Act notably prohibits discrimination by covered employers on the basis of race, color, religion, sex or national origin.

While I was a student at Vallejo Junior High School in 1968, and four years after the federal legislative implementation of the Civil Rights Act of 1964, two black psychologists, William Henry Grier and Price Cobbs, collaborated on a book entitled Black Rage. In the book, they clinically presented from a medical mental-health perspective that Black people living in a racist, white supremacist society were still being psychologically damaged by the still ongoing effects of racist oppression.

While I was living in Arizona in the 1980's, I once attended a talk given at Arizona State University by the notably renowned black professor of psychiatry from Harvard Medical School, Dr. Alvin Poussaint, a discussion in which he covered the continuing problematic aspects that even successful and renowned black professional people in the mental health field such as himself, along with and successful black people in general, face daily while living within a white and oppressively racist American culture.

It has always been a fairly easy and non-resistant proposition for educated white individuals to lead, or in particular, mislead, ignorantly bigoted white people. Most ignorant racist white folk, as a rule, generally don't care about the moral, or ethical basis of what they're being instructed to believe and follow; they just want the end result to be one which remains locked in their favor. Some American corporations deliberately hire, keep and promote white supremacist racists to behave in a racially discriminating manner, and then insist that these hired agents of bigotry publicly pretend as if the whole world, or in particular, after having chosen a few of their selected "favorite" black employees, to also pretend, and state "for the record" that they were ALL actually "color blind" to the true intent of their racially bigoted oppressive actions.

It was, therefore, not totally surprising then, that the ignorant, racist bigots from the neighboring San Francisco Bay Area communities surrounding the Vallejo CA home office headquarters of the TIMEC Corporation, chose to ignore the beautiful and truly diverse, multicultural societal reality of Vallejo, CA, the former home of the Mare Island Naval Shipyard, which is also known as the most racially diverse city in the United States of America.

Writing this book has been, for me, an emotionally taxing catharsis. I feel its creative existence to be vital in order for me to be able to actually complete a previously stated goal I proclaimed after the federal court civil rights trial victory pertaining to this matter, which was to further the process of "moving on with my life". You may very well likely notice, as you read along, that my writing style as I move through the stages and incidents of this sometimes painful recantation will often gradually digress to a presentation which will appear, in print, as a scattered and emotional rant. Completing this book would not have been possible if I hadn't allowed myself the writer's luxury of "strapping myself into the moment", and "surging through" quite a few of these painfully remembered experiences. For this literary breaking away from "proper", structured, American English writing, while oftentimes and frequently breaking from point to point I, in advance, ask for your understanding, and truly, humbly apologizes. Thank you.

Chapter 1

~Attorney Brent Babow~

Educated individual and attorney Brent Babow, who was the General Legal Counsel of the TIMEC Company during the time frame covered here of 1993 thru 1998, had earned his Bachelor's degree in Economics from the University of California at Davis, and his law degree from Hastings College of the Law, before being admitted to the California Bar in 1985. As TIMEC's General Legal Counsel, it was attorney Babow's responsibility to set the legal and ethical scheme, and theme, of the TIMEC Corporation's interactions with society in general. I was, in December of 1993, an occasional TIMEC employee approaching the chronological age of 40 years, hoping to impress someone in authority with my work ethic; just the same as every other TIMEC worker. My goal was to work enough hours in one year to "qualify" for full-time employment status, which would then allow me to be "eligible" for their benefit package. I have educationally, subsequent to my adventure with the TIMEC Company, gone on to earn an Associate's degree in Paralegal Studies from Phoenix Community College, in Phoenix, AZ, in the Maricopa County Community College District (MCCCD).

In his book <u>The Alchemist</u>, author Paulo Coelho wrote, in describing the boy Santiago's inner-perspective concerning the sheep he led, "If I became a monster today, and decided to kill them, one by one, they would become aware only after most of the flock had been slaughtered...." That passage, in my opinion, very much describes the potential for despair which can be imposed by a workplace group-think policy which willfully misrepresents its stated goals and purposes.

Racial relations in the American workplace have painfully, but slowly, evolved since the end of slavery. The resistance to actual workplace equality generally finds its operational matrix in the minds, and in the hands of, racist white people who are, for whatever reason, at least subconsciously lingering for a nostalgic return to this nation's

13

black-vs.-white past.   These people, then in turn have become presently reluctant to currently live in a truly open and diverse society. In 1993, The TIMEC Company of Vallejo, CA, recklessly placed its public image of racial relations into the hands of a duplicitous and dishonest human resource department which became entwined with a myopic, cost-driven risk management administration, who were then both led and directed by an unethical corporate general legal counsel before subsequently merging and evolving to become a formidable troika roadblock obstruction on the road to societal growth and diverse cultural expansion. As a paralegal, I am now so very much more clear, pointedly aware and knowledgeable, of the actual, blatant, medical/legal-ethical violations involved in what licensed attorney Brent Babow, on behalf of the TIMEC Company, actually did to me, all in an ignorant and bigoted collective effort with his administrative cohorts by brazenly attempting to bully me, through litigation, into silently allowing them to steal two and one-half hours of overtime from me.

Racism in the American workplace can serve to be a costly form of corporate ignorance. While white racists in supervisory positions of decision-making power, who are publicly reluctant to openly admit that they are indeed racist white supremacists surprisingly, and with frequent patterns, leave very clear tell-tale trails of documentary evidence of their racially-biased personnel decisions. Their private communications, and whispers amongst each other, then abruptly become confusing for them to accurately recall, even for the deceptive purpose of inaccurately recalling them with the accurate precision needed, for during their court-ordered depositions.

Oil refineries in America are very dangerous places to work. For a person to become skilled at working safely in an oil refinery environment, one must absolutely commit to becoming vigilant in their cognitive awareness of their environment at all times. What they hear, what they smell, and where they step, and/or stand becomes vitally important to always notice. Which hose is for air pressure, which one for nitrogen, and which aperture makes the water hose a different tool altogether becomes significant, along with what they perceive about even the atmospheric temperature in the very air of their work space area. How to instantly be able to perceive the air

14

pressure, water pressure, temperature, and flow rate viscosity of the surrounding petroleum byproducts, along with recognizing the substantive differences between asphalt, wax, fuel oil, light ends, gasoline and propylene. Dealing on a daily basis with the alternatingly disgusting and competing stomach-turning smells, of sulfur gas and ethyl mercaptan, while always looking out for the flags and yellow and red tape which point out the dangerous areas where odorless gases which can immediately kill exists. Doing this work provides a respectable contribution to our American society; while always realizing that a mere gallon of propane explodes with the force of thirteen sticks of dynamite, and that becoming unexpectedly trapped in a small cloud of anhydrous ammonia can instantly and powerfully constrict a person's lungs, totally taking away one's capacity to breathe either in, or out.

One always finds one's thought process alternating between working hard and working carefully, while always remembering within one's inner-reality of understanding that a simple spark of static electricity to a faulty compressor, or a latent spark, errantly generated from an ungrounded loading hose, can set off a loud, or even silent, fiery explosion which has the capacity to immediately send a person into the afterlife in a fireball.

Oil refinery work is a very dangerous, occupation, indeed; it is also work which is clearly too dangerous to have to be forced to simultaneously be on guard to contemplate, and work through, the dangerous ignorance of racist bigotry while dealing with the instinctive aspects of survival.

Some injuries are, of course, caused by an errant worker's own personal and careless neglect. Often, for these employees, their persistent and ongoing sophomoric reluctance, or refusal to take advantage of, their employer's stated and directed safety rules and company policies, leads to their constant ignoring of the obvious importance for Personal Protective Equipment (PPE), which leaves them open to be scarred and maimed; fingers, eyes, and toes are sometimes immediately lost, because hard-hats, gloves, goggles and steel-toed shoes are, at various times during the work shift, considered to be optional by distracted "eager to please" employees.

15

Back injuries, joint injuries and the psychological stress categories of workplace injuries, are referred to, on a medical-legal basis by risk-management administrators, as "soft injuries". A "soft-tissue injury" in a person's back (spinal column), or in their joints (the location where two or more bones make contact) are subjectively perceived injuries which are first known and acknowledged by the injured party. These painful injuries often do occur, however, in the witnessed presence of co-workers. The third and also subjectively acknowledged soft injury, psychological, or psychiatric stress injuries, can of course also occur while being actually witnessed by co-workers. In 1995, within the California Workers' compensation Code, there existed a new caveat in section (b)(1) of California Labor Code § 3208.3 concerning psychiatric injuries which stated that: "In order to establish that a psychiatric injury is compensable, an employee shall demonstrate by a preponderance of the evidence that actual events of their employment were predominant as to all causes combined of the psychiatric injury." Therefore, it clearly became more incumbent upon a psychiatric stress injured worker to prove and establish that they were actually psychologically injured more by the actual events at work, than by any other cause.

A "soft" workplace injury is one whereby the injured party's opinion of the degree of said pain determines the level and time frame term of the treatment necessary in order to fully recover. A competent and responsible risk-management administrator should always be on the lookout for "shamming", or the faking of the symptoms of soft injuries, which can prolong treatment, extend time off from work, and simultaneously result in a financial windfall for the deceptive worker. Can the effects of a psychiatric injury be misrepresented by an injured worker? I suppose so; for example, employee survivors of violent workplace trauma such as shootings, or armed robberies, can certainly and clearly be affected to varying degrees, according to what each individual personally and actually witnessed and/or experienced. The facts of such an unfortunate occurrences would then, without a doubt, need to be painfully examined carefully and thoroughly.

It would then seem, however, that an actual and thorough examination of the real facts, or "actual events criteria" involved in my psychiatric injury, which was alleged to have been based upon workplace racial

16

discrimination would have been an absolute requirement for an effective medical diagnosis to occur in determining the actual extent and degree to which I had actually been injured. It would also have made clear and easy sense to ascertain that my situation could have been, as it absolutely and undoubtedly was, severely compounded and exasperated when the TIMEC Company deliberately worked very hard, and at great financial expense to, in the alternative, attempt to illicitly hide, and shape, the actual facts surrounding my psychiatric injury, as they selfishly and with malice created their own self-serving, and illegitimate fictional account of the actual events involved. They obviously simply did not care anything at all about the lingering impact their racist actions would, and did have, upon my psyche as a black man. Welcome now, to what actually became my war.

Chapter 2

~The Prelude~

On December 3, 1993, while employed by the TIMEC Company, Inc. I attended a company-sponsored class entitled "Legal Issues for Supervisors". This class was offered as one part of a series of Supervisory Training classes, which also included "Timekeeping" and "Safety Issues" for individuals who someday desired to run TIMEC crews by minimally attaining the status of "Foreman B". During this particular Legal Issues section of the training class package, we were cautioned to understand that, at the status of "Foreman B", we were also expected to anticipate being the frontline of defense regarding any TIMEC employee legal claims. We learned to apply the implementation of the preferred TIMEC corporate way of investigating complaints and claims which TIMEC employees might make regarding their claims of racial and sexual harassment and discrimination; thereby, as a part of the evening's instruction primer, we became clearly and broadly well-versed on the legal definitions of, and technical legal distinctions between, harassment and discrimination.

Gary French, the TIMEC Company president, was in attendance at the Legal Issues class, observing the educational proceedings, while TIMEC Corporation General Counsel Brent Babow instructed and directed the group. Babow shared, from an attorney's perspective, the written and prepared TIMEC corporation policy and procedure materials, while we practiced role-playing. We learned how to tirelessly inquire of imaginary claimants during imaginary investigations, every anticipated and perceived nuance by repeatedly asking, over and over, "Is there anything else?" We were also instructed and warned to be sure to take copious investigative notes so as to fully and completely document every possible instance of everything, for "the record", which was to become part of the TIMEC corporation official legal position of defense to any complaints. It was told to us, as a group, that it was important to be able to establish, in writing and on paper, that "from the outset" every complaint had received serious contemplative review. Yes, indeed, the theme of that evening was, "Documentation, documentation and documentation".

However, what I initially failed to notice, before eventually coming to fully understand subsequently, as I sat through the company presentation that evening, was that as a white man, TIMEC General Counsel Brent Babow was a repressive corporate racist bigot; and that the unseen component of the policy creed which he was working so diligently at explaining, in behest of establishing TIMEC Corporation interests, did not hold any promise of justice or fair play for me as an African American man. The company policy he presented was a snake's policy, which also discretely held that nowhere in the entire catalogue of policies and practices which he was promoting, protecting and defending as their attorney, and nowhere in any aspect of any mission of the TIMEC corporation Administrative offices which he was directing and overseeing at that time did he, Brent Babow, in any way, as a licensed member of the California Bar, intend for me as a black male TIMEC Corporation employee, to ever receive any form of any benefit or protection of any of these TIMEC corporate policies or practices which were being discussed that evening, or of any benefits or protections properly held as law under any other provision of any California state law, or of any employee protection laws set in place to support and achieve that legally required protection under the federal laws of the United States of America.

The subsequent events and bad actions committed, and overseen by, attorney and TIMEC General Counsel Brent Babow made a mockery of that December 3, 1993 Legal Issues "training session"; however, I must now give due credit to Babow for dragging me, despite my reluctance, into an introduction with the true conceptual oxymoron of racial labor law ethics, which was thereby fiercely imposed upon me, by his overzealous over-employing of punitive and abusive litigation tactics. His folly eventually provided the spark of provocation for my seeking a proactive defensive education of all things pertaining to the legal industry of Employment Law. My quest for knowledge and understanding would then ultimately and cumulatively develop into an expansion within my conscious mind as it became a permanent part of my physical and psychological identity. I must now move along with this official and true storytelling, while I proceed to share with you my perspective as to how this evolution all came about. All

19

of the basic pertinent legal-issue facts, names of people, and renditions of incidents I shall mention and describe here are on file as a matter of public record, and are thereby absolutely verifiable through case file legal research of the public entities mentioned herein.

In mid-September of 1994, I was assigned by the TIMEC corporation to work as a "Mechanic A" with their contracted standing maintenance crew at the Shell Oil Refinery in Martinez, CA. I was the only African-American TIMEC worker assigned to that crew, at that pay rate, during that time frame. The job was a standard 40 hour per week assignment, with very little overtime available;...I soon noticed, however, that during the same time frame, TIMEC's contract maintenance site at the Unocal Oil Refinery in nearby Crockett-Rodeo CA had a larger, and more extensive work project going on, due to an August 1994 Unocal accidental refinery chemical-cloud release, whereby additional workers from TIMEC's Shell-Martinez, CA Refinery maintenance site were also being utilized over at Unocal Crockett-Rodeo CA in an overtime capacity on weekends. I had informed TIMEC Shell-Martinez maintenance crew Supervisor John Allen that I desired to be considered eligible and available to work the extra hours at Unocal, but never was I ever included in his selection of workers to go over to that refinery for the weekend overtime. Consequently, the only overtime opportunities available for me at that time would be those I could pick up at the TIMEC Shell-Martinez refinery maintenance site. With my employee designation as "Mechanic A", I had a job-skill set which allowed me to work at pipefitter/boilermaker, scaffolding and insulation assignments. I also drove the forklift and did light crane work, and I frequently reminded, and let all my TIMEC-Shell co- workers know, that if any situation came up for me to get a few extra hours, they should please and directly let me know.

Subsequently, during one September, 1994 afternoon at TIMEC Shell maintenance, a Shell Oil Refinery operations technician requested that some filter sets be changed out at his unit. Myself, and another, white, TIMEC Mechanic A contractor, Mike Tam, were assigned to the task by TIMEC-Shell maintenance crew Supervisor John Allen;.....by the end of the shift, the Shell oil refinery technician had been so much satisfied and thoroughly impressed by the speed and efficiency with which the two of us had completed the change-out task, that he made TIMEC the offer of allowing us to change all of the filters out in a continuing overtime project for that day.

That offer of an overtime assignment would have been welcome news for me, had I only been allowed to hear it. A real problem was subtly developing however, in that TIMEC's Shell maintenance crew Supervisor John Allen had chosen, instead and behind my back, to give my portion of the earned overtime opportunity to a different, white, maintenance crew worker friend of his, Rodney Barbush, without even telling me that this overtime opportunity was available.

I never would have known about this overtime theft and deception, had it not been for a TIMEC-Shell maintenance crew co-worker who stopped me to verbally chastise me as we were preparing to leave for the day by saying, "I don't get you, John, man...all that whining you've been doing about wanting overtime, and now, there you are, turning down the overtime which was available on your own job!"

At first, I couldn't believe what I had just heard. Every individual TIMEC employee knew that if a job you were working on went into overtime, the responsibility for fulfilling the overtime job task was yours, unless you personally asked, and were allowed to be, excused from working it. I hadn't turned down anything. I immediately became incensed and livid with smoldering rage; I knew I was going to have to work very hard to struggle to compose myself.

Suddenly and inwardly, every perceived direct and indirect slight, every subdued racist pronouncement and murmur I had ever overheard, and every incident whereby an ignorant, illiterate, bigoted and racist buffoon was placed in authority over my work-product while I, in turn, had never been allowed to ever run any crew, at any time was rushing, in full Technicolor, to the forefront of my conscious mind. I absolutely had to express my verbal complaint to somebody, right there and then, or bust. I had to vent; this was not right. It was wrong, so very wrong on so many levels. I went looking for TIMEC crew Supervisor John Allen; he was not in his office.

I went into the break garage looking for him, the place where we assembled for crew meetings. There, I saw TIMEC Foreman Jeff Thomasson sitting at the lunch bench. I approached him and chose my words very carefully. I could feel my chest pounding with my heart, lungs and stomach trembling as I took in a deep breath and began to slowly and directly speak. "What sense does it make", I asked, "for me to bust my ass doing a maintenance job well enough to earn an overtime opportunity, only to get aced out of that overtime behind my back by my own co-worker?." I got it said, exhaled, and stood my ground as I maintained eye contact with him while I waited for his official response. He began to stammer, while looking down and beginning to roll his head, when, from upstairs in the garage, a loud, booming and directly authoritative voice rudely interrupted our exchange with the firm pronouncement, "It means that you might get to stay around here for another week!"

The voice belonged to TIMEC's head man in charge at Shell Martinez; it was the voice of TIMEC's Yosemite Sam look-a-like, Shell Martinez Oil Refinery site Superintendent, Geno Kitsch. The statement he had just made was, without a doubt, an overtly voiced threat of attempted intimidation. The message clearly directed to me was that if I intended to be allowed to keep working at that particular job site, I was going to have to understand and accept the reality that unfair, racial discriminatory treatment was going to be "part of the drill", and a burden I would be required to submit to, without complaint, whenever TIMEC deemed it necessary.

I was shocked, stunned, and speechless. I literally could not say another word. I gathered my belongings and left for the day. As I drove home, I began to feel and realize the true extent to which I had just been insulted. First of all, for TIMEC-Shell Oil Refinery Superintendent Geno Kitsch to, with all blatant and direct hubris, publicly threaten me by attempting to instill a stoic spirit of fear within me, was ludicrously ridiculous. In addition, racially discriminating against me by taking money out my pocket was in direct opposition to federal law, and I knew it. I also knew that the TIMEC Corporation knew it, as well.

As my mind searched for a practical reason for Geno's action, I became somewhat inwardly delusional, telling myself, "It was a test, it had to be a test….It could not have been real". My mind then began to take a protective inventory: "Grown men didn't openly speak to each other that way….he could not really have been insinuating that I would have to save myself, and my job, by suspending reality and all rational thought…..He certainly could not have been directly speaking to me publicly in such a manner that openly revealed his personal opinion of me to be somehow less than that of a human being; and he absolutely certainly could not have been waiting for me to actually sanction that opinion of his with a public and verbal submissive reply of compliance"…..not just to steal two and one-half hours of overtime from me.

Everyone in the TIMEC Corporation I had ever worked for or with, including that particular TIMEC-Shell Superintendent, Geno Kitsch, knew that I had eagerly performed every single job-related task TIMEC had ever asked me to do. I had taken and attended, on my own time, every single job-skill improvement class which had been offered to TIMEC employees. Every job summation review I had ever received was exemplary. I had not ever been accused or charged with doing anything wrong, on any job site, at any time. So then, whatever could it possibly have been, aside from the color of my skin, which made TIMEC feel the unyielding need to treat me in such a despicable manner that day?

I then had a dreadful consideration cross my mind as I wondered to myself, "What are they really trying to make me do?" I quickly and immediately recognized, realized, and rejected the self-destruct notion. I KNEW that physically acting out would be insane, and furthermore, I absolutely do not ever intend to go to jail because of dealing with ignorant, foolish bigots. I also remembered that during that very day, and throughout every work shift, I had always and absolutely done my very best to treat all of my TIMEC co-workers as fellow human beings; and that was basically all I had ever expected from them in return.

For the white racist bigots of TIMEC-Shell maintenance to establish a hostile work environment by publicly and out loud personally not liking me, or black people in general, was clearly and illegally racial harassment; however, that sort of harassment was something with which I had unfortunately become acquainted with and accustomed to. It was an issue which I could, and already had been, on a daily basis, working around, with, and through. However, and in stark, dark contrast, my personal "line in the sand" was that the racist regime at TIMEC-Shell maintenance most certainly was not going to be allowed to steal my money from me with my blessing, not ever; not even one dime.

The TIMEC Corporation then, as a matter of legal principle (which I had learned from them), was absolutely going to have to publicly chastise TIMEC-Shell Superintendent Geno Kitsch for speaking the way he did to me, and in addition, right there, then and forevermore, choose to remove their thieving-hand policy from my pocket. TIMEC, as a corporation, was going to have to make it clear to me that they understood and accepted the reality that they were not ever going to be allowed to take from me what they know is mine, and that trying to bully-force me with intimidating innuendo to submit to accepting those terms as a condition of employment was forevermore totally unacceptable.

Taking money from me on racist terms was a truly unlawful criminal act, and also was clearly defined as illegal racial discrimination under their own stated terms, according to and based upon attorney and TIMEC General Counsel Brent Babow's own teachings of his own TIMEC's corporate "Legal Issues for Supervisors" class materials. I stopped off to get a bite to eat, and as I made it through the standing line at the Asian restaurant, I decided, right then and there, that it was time for me to find out if the TIMEC Company president Gary French and TIMEC General Counsel Brent Babow really meant what they were saying when they taught that class.

Chapter 3

~Hand-Written Complaint~

That night, in September of 1994, I prepared a hand-written complaint of racial discrimination on a lined half-sheet of notebook paper. In the letter of complaint, I made sure to mention that I felt TIMEC's actions had overtones of racial discrimination. This particular phrasing would require that TIMEC immediately investigate the circumstances involved from a corporate administrative level. Because I was also complaining about the TIMEC-Shell Martinez, CA site Superintendent Geno Kitsch, the letter was required to be delivered to someone impartial, who had actual authority over him. We had been instructed, during the Safety Issues component of the Supervisory Training Courses, that Safety Issues superseded every other workplace concern, so therefore, when I observed TIMEC's corporate Safety Superintendent Jim Jerge on site as I arrived for work the next morning, I chose to hand him a copy of the complaint. (I, of course, kept the original for my own records, "just in case").

A few days later, Barry Raymos, the TIMEC corporate Director of Human Resources arrived at the Shell maintenance site, presumably, as I was told, to get my "official" statement "for the record". I admit that I was curious about how the TIMEC corporation chain of command was going to work through this now-official situation. Geno Kitsch the TIMEC Shell Martinez site Superintendent who had threatened me and, Raymos, the TIMEC Human Resource (HR) Director were longtime friends who had worked together for a very long time. Both Superintendent Kitsch and TIMEC Shell maintenance crew Supervisor John Allen had been featured as being out of line in my written complaint. HR Director Raymos invited me to take a ride on site in his car. There, I explained what I felt had happened, and afterwards he said that he would be getting back with me after he completed his investigation.

A basic and proper investigation of my racial discrimination complaint would have revealed at its inception, just by looking at the TIMEC-Shell maintenance hazard analysis sheets for the day in question, that I, along with another TIMEC-Shell maintenance employee, most certainly did perform the filter-changing task during regular day shift hours on that date. A further and proper review, of the TIMEC-Shell maintenance time-keeping records for that same day, would have instantly shown that the same job, indeed, had provided two and one-half hours of TIME-Shell maintenance for two TIMEC-Shell maintenance employees. Also, the time records would reveal that I, John Bumphus, a black TIMEC employee, had been surreptitiously excluded from the overtime opportunity, and replaced by a different, white, TIMEC-Shell maintenance employee by the name of Rodney Barbush. My written and delivered complaint of racial discrimination therefore was valid, and indeed had merit. All that was needed was for an actual investigation to have taken place. In addition, I was also looking forward very eagerly and willingly to officially confronting Geno Kitsch face-to-face, anytime and anyplace, in front of Barry Raymos, or anyone else in an official position within the TIMEC Corporation, about his attempted intimidation of me.

On the next day after the day TIMEC Human Resources Director Barry Raymos had stopped by the TIMEC-Shell job site to speak with me during his investigation of my written complaint of racial discrimination, TIMEC-Shell site Superintendent Geno Kitsch, during the weekly TIMEC-Shell maintenance crew safety meeting, took out some time to personally and directly address a "problem", which he termed as, "the matter of the people who think that TIMEC owes them something". Geno went on to inform the assembled group that "those people" were not team players, and that they would not ever be the ones chosen for promotional advancement within the TIMEC Corporation. I clenched my teeth, kept my composure, and just continued looking him straight into his eyes while he was speaking, as I blankly ignored his heavy innuendo, which did everything except call me by name.

I silently mused to myself that he was going to look real silly, when it came time for him to explain what he meant by using the words he had chosen to try to intimidate me earlier, along with also having to explain what he meant by saying what he saying right then, at that time, to our collected group. Yes indeed, in my opinion at that time,

Geno Kitsch was certainly digging a big hole for himself with his caustic way of publicly speaking. I was, on that day, even more determined to let the investigation into his actions as a TIMEC Superintendent take its full and complete course.

However,......the UGLY fact, which did not become publicly revealed until over three years later, in the San Francisco Federal District Courthouse of Judge Susan Illston, was that TIMEC corporation Human Resources Director, Barry Raymos, had by that time already shredded my presented written complaint, along with all, if there ever were any, notes pertaining to any racial discrimination investigation. His official "investigation" visit, therefore, had really been no more than someone's ignorant and ham-fisted plan of an illegal, and insultingly placating, dodge; a perfunctory ruse designed to obfuscate and stultify my quest for justice.

For Human Resource Director Barry Raymos to have ignorantly and secretly conspired within the insidious TIMEC Corporation plan to shred my heartfelt handwritten complaint of racial discrimination was, at that time, a totally unexpected occurrence. Truthfully, I had actually expected to receive some form of blow-back from various unknown factions within the TIMEC workforce crew for being "the guy who told on Geno"; that expectation was due to the reality that subservient slave-sheep have historically not initially appreciated anyone ever causing grief to their beloved "massa". However, the apparently forgotten and/or ignored TIMEC Company administrative truth was that I HAD ACTUALLY DONE THE ABSOLUTELY CORRECT THING by bringing the racial discrimination of TIMEC-Shell maintenance crew Supervisor John Allen, and the subsequent intimidation attempt by TIMEC-Shell site Superintendent Geno Kitsch into the open BEFORE taking my complaint to the federal government. TIMEC was not ever going to be able to make the reality of my written complaint "go away". This realization was based upon what I had actually learned during the TIMEC Supervisory Training classes which had been taught by their own TIMEC corporate General Counsel and their own TIMEC corporate Safety Superintendent. They were not going to be allowed to intimidate me into silently accepting their maltreatment without complaint, as I was intent upon bringing the matter to the full attention of all TIMEC corporate administrators. I had certainly, I'll admit, "put it all on the line" for, and with, the TIMEC corporation, "in house". All due to what I erroneously but sincerely believed was a collective form of "us". And I had done it for the sake of what had been preached to all TIMEC employees about the necessity of always working from a "team" concept. Now, let's get back to the story.

After being laid off from the TIMEC-Shell maintenance job in mid-October, 1994, I found myself, with great and pronounced naivety, still impatiently waiting, on and throughout November and December of 1994, for Barry Raymos, TIMEC's Director of Human Resources, to officially reveal the results of his investigation pertaining to my written racism complaint of September 1994; results which were never going to appear. I had then also become very eager, during this waiting period as a now-disgruntled TIMEC employee, to review the actual Collective Bargaining Agreement (CBA) which our union, the International Union of Petroleum and Industrial Workers (IUPIW) had signed with TIMEC. All my requests to the TIMEC Corporation offices for a personal copy of our current-at-that-time labor contract had been deftly side-stepped or summarily ignored. When I asked them for the name of my union shop steward, I was told that it was Jeff Thomasson, (the TIMEC-Shell Foreman I was complaining to when Geno Kitsch threatened me). However, I had also been advised and directed by another TIMEC temporary co-worker towards the National Labor Relations Board (NLRB) as a possibility for resolving the issue. I actually had thought that the NLRB might have a copy on file for me.

After multiple visits to the federal NLRB office in Oakland, CA, in early January of 1995, the NLRB intake officer told me to go to TIMEC's corporate office and once again, formally request a copy of the current CBA. For some reason, that time it worked. What I found in the document upon review profoundly disturbed me. The CBA revealed that the cowardly racist TIMEC-Shell maintenance site Supervisor John Allen, whom I had directly accused of racial discrimination for stealing my overtime in my September, 1994, complaint letter to TIMEC had somehow been placed as a member of the union employee's contract negotiating team. I was totally perplexed as to how in the world a practicing TIMEC corporation company bigot Supervisor could be allowed, or expected to, for that matter, genuinely represent the interests of a union-dues paying employee during a Collective Bargaining Agreement negotiation?

Chapter 4

~Patience Is Wearing Thin~

On January 18, 1995, my patience regarding waiting for Barry Raymos to contact me about the findings of his investigation was wearing very thin. Upon being reassigned by TIMEC in mid-January to the TIMEC-Chevron Oil Refinery industrial maintenance site in Richmond, CA, I spoke with TIMEC-Chevron site Superintendent Dave Newman regarding my concerns over the lack of an official response of resolution to my written complaint of racial discrimination. I explained the whole TIMEC-Shell racial discrimination overtime debacle story to Dave Newman, in great detail. I also told him about the newfound absurdity I had just recently discovered regarding TIMEC-Shell Supervisor John Allen being on the union employee's contract negotiating committee.

On January 19, 1995, after working the morning half of my day shift assignment, I came to the realization that I was so wrapped up in my emotional preoccupation pertaining to my racial discrimination complaint not being resolved, and in my rage and distress over waiting so long to hear from the TIMEC corporate administrators about what was going to happen to Geno Kitsch for the way he had spoken to me in September of 1994, that it actually was becoming a dangerous workplace attention distraction which could potentially evolve into a work-place safety liability. I was, obviously, much more than just pissed off. Therefore, responsibly, I spoke again with TIMEC-Chevron Oil Refinery industrial site Superintendent Dave Newman at his office and requested to be allowed to go home early that day, with the understanding that if I was not going to be able to maintain focus enough to apply myself to the job by the next morning, I would report in as being ill. Dave Newman told me that he understood my dilemma, and had no problem with my proposal; however, he also added that there was one more "little thing" which needed to be taken care of. Apparently my name, for the very first time during my employment with TIMEC, had come up for random drug screen testing.

After I complied with the urine screen and left the TIMEC-Chevron job site, I immediately drove to my parent's home in Vallejo CA, where I was informed that a telephone message had been left for me from TIMEC, informing me that due to a work-force reduction pertaining to the job I was working on that day at Chevron, I had now been officially laid off from work. So, there was then no need for me to "check in" the next morning. I immediately called TIMEC-Chevron Superintendent Dave Newman and personally verified the message, before subsequently notifying the California Employment Development Department (EDD) that I had been laid off from work, so as to apply, establish my eligibility for, and receive Unemployment Insurance benefits, as was my right and expectation to so do.

Due to the fact that Barry Raymos had still not contacted me regarding my September 1994, complaint of racial discrimination by February 1, 1995, I began to realize that without professional mental health assistance, I was going to have considerable difficulty with handling my rage effectively enough to properly apply myself as a productive team member on the next call-out job for the TIMEC Company. The main thing causing me to hesitate seeking help was the unknown specter of the anticipated psychological medical costs. Over the previous five years of my working with TIMEC, I had not worked enough hours in any one of them for me to be able to have acquired their medical or health insurance benefit package. I was also feeling, with a slight sense of dread, that I had already verbalized perhaps too much detail about my personal displeasure over the TIMEC-Shell racism situation with TIMEC-Chevron Superintendent Dave Newman. Other than my Unemployment Insurance benefits, I had no current and immediately substantial income prospects available at that time. And unless TIMEC somewhat quickly called me back to work on another job, I would have no way of even making a down payment on a treatment series. In addition, I had no idea at all of what the cost of mental health counseling therapy could possibly be.

After asking around a bit among some friends of mine, I was eventually given the phone number of psychologist Dr. Ira Polonsky PhD., whose office was, comfortably, right in the Vallejo, CA, neighborhood where I had grown up. During my initial telephone interview with him it became clear to me that I could in no way

AFFORD to pay for a treatment series, and that even if I could come up with the involved cost, Dr. Polonsky had a very busy schedule between multiple Bay Area offices. It would be very difficult to ever even get in for an appointment. So imagine my genuine surprise, amazement and gratitude when the good doctor called back and informed me that he would, indeed, see me the next day, and that we could work out an affordable payment plan for his services.

My decision to seek professional mental health assistance in February of 1995 was borne out of the reality that my frustration, and severely pent-up rages, of righteous indignation about TIMEC's failure and refusal to respond to my legitimate and written complaint about blatant racial discrimination were causing me to, inwardly, begin having what I felt where becoming uncontrollable and vengeful over-the-top daydreams and fantasies of retribution; and I did not like the feeling of being afraid of myself.

On February 2, 1995, I met for the first with psychologist Dr. Ira Polonsky PhD. After I shared my story and told him my perceived issues, he concluded and shared with me that from his viewpoint, a large portion of my dismay concerning my ordeal was caused by the fact that I had actually and totally trusted and believed in the concept of TIMEC, as an entity; and that now I was lost in anger because I now actually felt totally betrayed by that very same entity. This was certainly a breakthrough in perspective and understanding for me, and I felt it to be very true. I had totally bought in to what TIMEC was selling me, and all of us, as employees.

I had seen the framed, behind-the-glass copy of the "14 Management Principles of W. E. Deming" which TIMEC displayed in the lobby of their Administrative offices as if it were their public, and private, mantra. For those few years I had very worked hard at the precarious task of learning and acquiring the dangerous oil refinery industrial maintenance mechanical skills necessary to assist TIMEC in competing for market space in the refinery maintenance industry. And also in that vein, I had enthusiastically developed societal group-working skills which even went so far as to embrace the rights of ignorant bigots to exist in their own delusional diversity for the sake of "the team". All because I wholeheartedly believed, that I was working for an entity which understood, and appreciated, my efforts in helping them to achieve a successful and diverse group work collaboration. And now, while I had literally, and for months patiently waited, for my legitimate and written complaint issues of the actual occurrences of racial discrimination within that very same TIMEC Company to which I had painstakingly committed myself, to be heard, and properly addressed on the corporate level, I had summarily been simply left hanging, and slowly twisting in the wind; like in a new-age symbolic lynching. It was becoming vibrantly clear to me, that as of that point in time, I had absolutely received no TIMEC corporation official consideration leading towards resolution of the matter whatsoever.

Suddenly and awkwardly, at that moment, with that very little bit of an insightful help diagnosis from psychologist Dr. Ira Polansky, PhD, I suddenly felt inspired enough to get myself free to take off the mask of self-delusion, so as to dare to move beyond the imaginary inner circle of the TIMEC Corporation's in-house conflict resolution system. I had to prepare myself to face the realization that TIMEC wasn't really interested in the aforementioned pretentious public posing of the framed declarative poster of the 14 Total Quality Management Principles of W. Edwards Deming, which was conspicuously hanging in the foyer of their corporate office, clearly visible and on display to greet all current and prospective employees and visitors. Nor were they even pretending to be bound to the principles discussed in the their own "Legal Issues for Supervisor's Course" which TIMEC company President Gary French taught while legal General Counsel Brent Babow directed, on December 3, 1993, for employees who desired to run crews. I was starting to feel more and more unease, as it was beginning to be revealed to me, right then and there, that it very may well have all been a contrived and pretentious TIMEC Company corporate hoax. If justice was going to be found for me concerning my situation, I was obviously going to have to find it for myself.

Chapter 5

~Separation Anxiety~

On February 3, 1995, just like any other de-programmed individual suddenly seeing the light of day after being freed from the psychological oppression of a cult, I was starting to feel the beginning pangs of Separation Anxiety. I clearly knew that if I followed through, with the disruptive action of officially taking my complaints "out of house" and to the federal government, that I would then be admitting, and stating publicly for all the world to see, that I no longer trusted in TIMEC, or in the TIMEC corporation's stated, written and taught purported resolution policy of commitment to resolve my issues and perceptions of workplace racial discrimination. I was therefore immediately and at that moment going to have to resolve, and put in check, each and every one of my own hesitant inhibitions. I was going to have to choose to be fully committed as to whether I was going to accept the accompanying terms of war pertaining to this matter. I had to decide to be all in, in real time, to whistle-blow on the plague within the house of the TIMEC Corporation, or I would soon be forced to choose the alternative path of standing down and retreating from my aggressive position, scurrilously apologizing and begging for forgiveness. Turning against myself in self-sacrifice, while changing into a person sheepishly trying to accept responsibility for the dispute by declaring that "it was all my fault" and, of course, incessantly promising to do a better job at learning how to "go along to get along". It had certainly become "decision making time".

At that final juncture, on that day, I, of course, simply refused to "break weak" into a fit of cowardice. I had faith, acquired through my religious studies, that Jehovah God was with me and looking out for me, and I knew that I was certainly raised much better by my parents, and by the members of my community, than for me to succumb, tremble and submit to some bigot corporation's overblown sense of racist mendacity. I realized that for me to have been backed down, and into a corner, while being forced to stoically accept this unseemly, and emotionally brutal racist maltreatment by the TIMEC Corporation would, in effect, mean spiritually shrinking, forever; because I would also then, and in turn, be abandoning and leaving all current and future complaining about anything the TIMEC corporation would ever do to me, or to anyone else in while in my presence, alone and without hope of redress, forever. I then decided to shake off that irrationally timid hesitation, and proceed with filing a charge against TIMEC with the National Labor Relations Board (NLRB). It was then, at that moment, officially and however long this battle of resolution eventually was going to take, "ON".

Before I filed the charge, however, I decided to reach out first to Tom Rincon, the sitting union president of the International Union of Petroleum and Industrial Workers (IUPIW). Surprisingly, he dismissively, and with a condescending chuckle, after having collected my union membership dues from my TIMEC corporation paychecks for well over five years, personally declined to assist me, in any way whatsoever, while laughingly offering me the unsolicited cautionary advice that the owner of TIMEC, R. Briggs Wood, had "a whole lot of money."

It was then made very clear to me, by his flippant attitude, that this particular proliferation of a workplace scab union chapter, set forth by the IUPIW, easily merged with the "bricks without straw" corporate policies regarding the TIMEC Corporation labor force; as TIMEC employees forced to participate in this sham of a union, the concept of that same union actually standing up for our rights as American workers was never intentioned to be more than a perfunctory ruse. My union president had no concern about my being maltreated, whatsoever.

On February 7, 1995, after having filed the NLRB charge on February 3, 1995, I realized that if I was going to make a comprehensive legal argument in any official capacity based upon my work record, I was going to have to be appraised about what was actually in my TIMEC personnel file as an employee. I had found out from my initial bit of personal legal research that by law, TIMEC was required to provide me with copies of everything they had compiled about me which had ever transpired concerning me during my term of employment, upon my request, at any time. I therefore requested, and picked up, a copy of my complete employee file from TIMEC's business office.

However, while reviewing the contents of my file with TIMEC Corporation Human Resource Director Barry Raymos, I surprisingly discovered that there was no record of my hand-written September, 1994 complaint located in my copy of my file. I then and at that moment provided Barry Raymos with another copy, for them to have for THEIR record.

Also on February 7, 1995, TIMEC apparently received notice of my February 3, 1995, NLRB charge. They then in turn chose to on that date, in a successful illicit effort which actually got me sanctioned by the State of California Employment Development Department (EDD), to contact and falsely state to an EDD representative that I had been discharged from work on January 19, 1995, due to my not reporting for work because I had been in jail. Therefore, they were blatantly lying about me, with total and absolutely unsubstantiated malice; so as to scurrilously insinuate that I had fraudulently received unemployment insurance benefits.

In addition, on that February 7, 1995 date, I filed a civil rights discrimination complaint against the TIMEC Corporation with the California Department of Fair Employment and Housing (DFEH), in Oakland, CA, as a prelude requirement to my February 21, 1995, filing of a civil rights violation charge with the United States Equal Employment Opportunity Commission (EEOC).

Why the TIMEC Company would choose to take such a cowardly and ugly course of action against me at that time has never been explained to me. It was such a low-class move for a corporation that it still to this day tilts me toward feelings of anger and dismay. Even as I, post-litigation, and post-verdict, have bought the topic up in conversation with a person no longer primarily employed by TIMEC, all I received in response, was an unofficial rendering of the mendacious boilerplate lie known as, "No one ever deliberately tried to hurt you because of your race, John.", which was not, of course, not a truthful recounting of the events. The actual truth was that I had not been "laid off" on January 19, 1995, by a workforce reduction; I had actually, instead of having my complaint met and resolved under the auspices of their own conflict resolution system, been unlawfully discharged and secretly fired, without notice, in an ugly back-stab assassination, by the TIMEC Corporation, for complaining about racial discrimination. A covert war had been lodged in place against me, intent upon the overall destruction of my capacity to even be able to perceive my rights under TitleVII of the Civil Rights Act of 1964. The TIMEC Corporation's administrative in-house attorney, General Counsel Brent Babow, would go on to arbitrarily and capriciously lead and direct a TIMEC Company corporate effort to compile, and file for submission, knowingly false and sworn under oath, contradictory statements of various TIMEC official company positions while simultaneously suborning perjury by submitting knowingly false sworn declarations by TIMEC employees under oath in response to my California Workers' Compensation injury claim, also along with, and in responsive answer to, the preceding NLRB and EEOC charges I had already filed. Indeed, a virulent and sneaky, undeclared scorched-earth war was absolutely occurring against me. I soon noticed that TIMEC's official written positions and sworn declarations under oath in response to the NLRB were markedly different in detail to TIMEC's official written position and sworn declarations under oath in response to the EEOC. Both of these conflicting messages of perjury, mendacity and misinformation were directed by Brent Babow. This was the illicitly formulated legal mess which I was going to be required to wade through, all about stealing two and one-half hours of my overtime.

Chapter 6

~Legal System~

Access to the legal system has often had a direct bearing upon the quality of life we enjoy as American citizens. For most working people, traffic court is just about as much familiarity with the courts as we can comfortably bear. Therefore, understand that in February of 1995, when I subsequently received a lengthy, voluminous sanction-packet from the EDD at the mailing address of my parent's home, I was somewhat stunned, and left numb with disbelief while at the same time being partially paralyzed in fear. I was, according to the EDD, in very big trouble because, according to their records, I had not been laid off from work by TIMEC on January 19, 1995, as I had reported while filing for the Unemployment Insurance benefits I was at that time receiving. Their investigative finding, after telephonically interviewing me, and representatives of the TIMEC Corporation, was that I had actually been fired by TIMEC on January 19, 1995, after not reporting to work due to my being incarcerated in jail. Furthermore, and most significantly, due to the illicit nature of the fraud I had allegedly committed, I was thereby immediately sanctioned and absolutely ineligible to receive any EDD benefits whatsoever for a very long time.

Where in the world did THIS come from? This insidious, sneaky plan of the TIMEC Corporation was apparently to starve me out with a damnable lie, all to steal two and one-half hours of my overtime. After TIMEC had secretly fired me by laying me off from work on January 19, 1995, my rightly earned unemployment insurance benefits were absolutely all the income I had available to me in the world; yet the TIMEC Corporation illegally and fraudulently went on to take a shot at stealing them, also, as if they somehow had been made privy to some sort of unknown and secret "white man's right" which would allow them to take my only remaining money away from me, as well.

I felt at that moment as if the actual entire "weight of the system" had been pushed down upon my spirit, and set upon my very chest. I was informed in the notice that if I was going to choose to dispute the EDD finding, I would have to formally request a timely hearing before an Administrative Law Judge, in order to prevent the sanctions from going into full effect.

Entering that Spring season in the year of 1995, my entire legal technology arsenal consisted of me, long-hand-printing letters and symbols very carefully, on lined sheets of legal tablets. I had absolutely no idea at that time as to how to even attempt to turn a personal computer on. I went to the Vallejo, CA Public Library, so as to try to familiarize myself with the terms and phrases set forth in the sanctioning documentation. The librarian there informed me that acquiring an understanding of the actual listed California Code violations in my sanctioning by their quoted numbered statutes and nuanced variances would require a more extensive legal database than the one available at any public library. It was then and thereby suggested that I go to the Solano County Law Library, in Fairfield CA, where the actual legal texts used by lawyers are available to the public.

In 1995, the Solano County Law Library was located in the Solano County Courthouse building in Fairfield, CA. The library rooms inside actually looked a lot like the backdrop of those TV shows, like "LA Law", or "Law and Order", which featured legal themes. No one had to tell you to be quiet when you entered the law library office; you just FELT it in the glancing looks you received as you opened the door. Everyone there who was in search of legal information had very serious and somber looks on their faces. This was clearly not a playground; it was, in reality, a war room. No one whom I observed seemed to be doing legal research for recreational purposes. And with an instantly perceptible discernment I realized was that no one's personal law office could have held as many differentiating and diverse law books as the law library had for legal research. This was obviously the place where lawyers went, when they needed to know more than what was in the books in their personal office libraries. I slowly then began to understand that THIS place was actually the level playing ground; this was where the laws for EVERYTHING were kept. All laws, even the laws for the lawyers, and also of course, even the rules of law for the judges, themselves.

The reality of talking with the law librarian was, in effect, a reality of talking with a state government paid, objective, non-partial legal issue professional. She could, would and indeed did, answer a wide range of legal questions. She patiently directed me and others to the books covering the legal issues I was dealing with, but there was one line she which would never cross; like a referee with a ready whistle, she would not ever delve into the area of giving personal legal opinions or advice. The legal research protocol, for me, became to patiently and quietly stand in line in front of her desk until it was my turn to be assisted, and to then, explain to her what I was trying to find an understanding to, in as complete and cogent a manner as was possible. Bothering other patrons for information, whether they are attorneys, law students, or other lay people such as myself, was absolutely not allowed, as it was considered to be rude and boorish behavior.

By way of my learning the art of fighting my own legal battle, my interests and research instincts led me to quickly come to the understanding of two Latin legal terms. The first one was "pro se", which meant I was representing myself without the benefit of the professional legal assistance of a licensed attorney. The second Latin term was "prima facie", which described presented evidence which was so clear that "on the face of itself" in a legal dispute it could in fact be termed as indisputable. The Court, as the judge is called, is somewhat required to look very hard at the evidentiary presentation of a pro se litigant who is not well-versed in "legalese", or the way lawyers handle court matters, in order to see if that evidence is, in fact, "prima facie"; therefore, that inherent pro se edge is a valuable and precarious premium.

Truth is an irrevocable attendant to any pro se litigation presentation. Any lie, or any attempt by a pro se litigant to deceive the Court by twisting facts, would mean an immediate defeat. For prima facie evidence concerning my appeal before the Administrative Law Judge (ALJ) regarding my EDD sanctioning, I knew that I could prove with actual phone company records, that I had placed a phone call to the

TIMEC-Chevron job site on January 19, 1995, to confirm that I had, indeed, actually been laid off from that site on that day after leaving that afternoon. I also knew that since I had not been in jail, there could be no prima facie evidence presentation that I had been. I also knew that any credible TIMEC sign-in attendance timesheet or the TIMEC Hazard Analysis form for the job which I had worked that day on would verify my attendance at Chevron on that day in question.

My retired father had experience in being a part of resolving a racially discriminatory group advancement opportunity employment situation while working as a black man at Napa State Hospital. He advised me to remember, as he counseled me about the intellectual and emotional chaos involved with openly challenging a racist and hostile white employer that, "They may be better educated, but they're not necessarily smarter than you, John." TIMEC was starting to reveal their weaknesses by openly lying and continuing to revise their official positions for different bureaucratic encounters. I had just one stream of truth to accurately remember; they were so insistent upon bringing illicit thunder to my subconscious mind, that they would literally swear under oath to any false statement which they thought could conveniently fit each and every occasion.

Once the TIMEC Company realized that I was actually challenging the wrongly-placed EDD sanctions, they found themselves in the position of having to answer under oath a second additional NLRB charge I had placed against them. Their response in turn was to adjust the initial EDD lie of my being in jail into a now alternative fairy-tale which declared I had actually asked to be laid off from work, on January 19, 1995. To expand and attempt to legitimize their new story, they enlisted the now suddenly-sycophantic servitude of TIMEC Chevron Superintendent Dave Newman, who fraudulently signed a retroactively-dated sworn statement falsely affirming that I had, indeed, asked to be laid off from work on that day, due to stress. A representative of TIMEC, and I, were soon scheduled to be appearing before an Administrative Law Judge to resolve the EDD dispute over my sanctioning appeal. It was shaping up to appear that once there, they clearly intended to bulldoze me with a barrage of surprising, manufactured lies. This had quickly become a war; so I chose to attempt a pre-emptive strike.

Mr. McKee, the Supervising Office Manager of the local Vallejo, CA, EDD, always presented the professional bearing, image and deportment of a very seriously contemplative African-American man while directing and overseeing a very structured, disciplined and well-organized office environment. It was somewhat locally understood by all that his employees, and the public at large, were required to treat each other respectfully in all interactions in his office. I felt and believed him to be a fair man, so I took the chance of personally approaching him at his desk, carefully and courteously, while yet speaking directly to him with the truth of what I viewed then as my very precarious situation. I said to Mr. McKee, "On January 19, 1995, I asked for the afternoon off from work so as to compose myself and see if I was willing to make the effort the next day to continue the job at TIMEC-Chevron. By the time I got home, they had already called and said half of my crew had been laid off on that day, including myself. I called them back to verify the layoff, and the TIMEC-Chevron Superintendent in charge told me that it was indeed true that I had been laid off. I subsequently had reason to file a charge against TIMEC with the NLRB on February 3, 1995, and when TIMEC got notice of it on February 7, 1995, somebody called here (the EDD) and falsely reported I had defrauded your office to receive the Unemployment Insurance benefits I received after my layoff. In a later telephone interview by the EDD, TIMEC said I had been in jail when they laid me off, which I absolutely had not. Now that TIMEC has realized that I am going to fight the EDD sanctions, they have come up with a new, false written statement from the Superintendent at TIMEC-Chevron, which now states that I had asked to be laid off. Mr. McKee, he knows that he's deliberately lying by signing that statement; he knows that I only asked for that afternoon off."

Mr. McKee immediately went to his telephone and called TIMEC-Chevron Superintendent Dave Newman, whom he then asked directly whether, or not, I was laid off from work on the date in question. Then, very stupidly, and I must admit surprisingly, ignorant bigot TIMEC Chevron Superintendent Dave Newman, when realizing he was speaking to an African-American, retorted with a very disrespectful, "What the f---*** difference?" Mr. McKee excused me from his office while he explained to Dave Newman the actual significance of what the difference really was. After their conversation, Mr. McKee informed me that he was immediately removing all the illicit sanctions which had been applied against me, while simultaneously filing and placing an official EDD Notice of False Statement finding against the TIMEC Corporation which would go into THEIR permanent California EDD file.

The EDD hearing with TIMEC before the Administrative Law Judge (ALJ) subsequently went on as originally scheduled, even after the EDD sanctions which had been wrongly placed against me had been removed. TIMEC's Human Resource Director Barry Raymos appeared for the company as their sole representative at the hearing and was asked about the origin of the plethora of false statements which had been lodged by TIMEC against me, and with a smirk, pled ignorance; when all the while, and with all complicit degenerate duplicity, he was sitting there knowing, but certainly not revealing to the ALJ, or more importantly, to me, that he had already previously shredded my originally presented written complaint of racial discrimination, as he pretended to be confused, befuddled and unknowing, after his "fake" investigation into my legitimate complaint of workplace racial discrimination. All of this drama, just to steal two and one-half hours of overtime from me.

Chapter 7

~After The EDD~

Returning to the Law Library after escaping TIMEC's EDD assassination attempt, I settled in to try and discover what my future legal options actually were. My legal research had led me to understand that a few unexpected bonuses had occurred from TIMEC's sworn, but summarily false written statement from TIMEC-Chevron Superintendent Dave Newman which had been presented to the EDD. The phrasing of his official letter as a superintendent on behalf of the TIMEC Corporation clearly established that TIMEC had indeed officially, and in their own written corporate word recognized, and noticed me to have been, suffering from a work-related stress injury to the extent that I had become incapable of continuing work, on January 19, 1995. Establishing EDD disability eligibility only required my further being independently evaluated by California State licensed psychologist Nagui Achamalla, in addition to the diagnostic statement presented from my own personal psychologist, Dr. Polonsky. Therefore, I was then able to utilize my suddenly restored EDD benefits for the slightly more lucrative disability insurance payments instead of the usual unemployment insurance payment rate. And because I had clearly been drug tested by TIMEC-Chevron Superintendent Dave Newman before I left on that day, I was thereby also free to apply the sworn written acknowledgement of my having sustained a work-related injury before my January 19, 1995, departure from work, to file and establish a workers' compensation claim for a psychological stress injury under California Labor Code § 3208.3.

California Labor Code section 3208.3 allows a psychiatric injury to be compensable under the California Workers' Compensation Code, when it can be established that the medical-treatment requiring injury, occurred during, in, and because of, the course of employment activity. The Workers' Compensation Code also allowed that the TIMEC Corporation actually had medical jurisdiction for the first 30 days after acknowledging the injury. However, after utilizing their right to drug-test me as a worker with work-related stress injured on the job on January 19, 1995, which TIMEC-Chevron Superintendent Dave Newman certainly did, they should have immediately sent me directly to their choice of mental health professional, psychiatrist Dr. Donald H. Stanford MD, of Berkeley, CA, which they certainly did not. Instead, TIMEC "held the ball", and waited for me to file a March 13, 1995 claim for the injury which, at that time, TIMEC Corporation Risk Management Administrator Sue Evans swore she had no idea, or any evidence whatsoever, of having occurred. I had already and on my own previously self-diagnosed, searched for and located, negotiated a payment plan for treatment, and regularly been seeing my own psychologist, Dr. Ira Polonsky, Ph D., since February 2, 1995; and when I filed my Workers' Compensation Claim 41 days later, TIMEC had not in any way responded to their own February 7, 1995 acknowledgment of my January 19, 1995 injury in any medical-legal defense sense whatsoever, other than to choose to illegally commit fraud in their lying attempt to unjustifiably steal from me my earned right to Unemployment Insurance benefits.

Therefore, the medical-legal management of my injury claim was now indisputably mine to establish and maintain. By California State Workers' Compensation law, TIMEC's 30-day window of control over the medical treatment pertaining to my injury claim had expired in the midst of their folly. They had also forfeited their right to require me to be examined by their choice of mental health professional, unless they forced me to litigate a Workers' Compensation claim of an injury for which they had actually already officially drug-screened me.

TIMEC's Workers' Compensation insurance coverage status in 1995 was "Permissibly Self-Insured", or PSI. PSI status meant that by putting up a cash bond with the State of California, the TIMEC Corporation was allowed to handle their own Workers' Compensation claims, and to also avoid the cost of purchasing insurance from a Workers' Compensation insurance carrier. Sue Evans was designated by TIMEC to coordinate their work injury medical expense liabilities as their corporate Risk Management Claims Administrator. Ms. Evans, in my instance, chose to enlist the legal services of attorney Carlton H.A. Taber, Esq., of Schmitt, Morris, Bittner & Schmitt, of Oakland, CA, to coordinate their illegal denial my claim, in direct violation of the guidelines of TIMEC's PSI agreement with the State of California.

These three (3) following prominent evidentiary facts pertaining to my Workers' Compensation claim were always available to TIMEC corporation Risk-Management Administrator Sue Evans, who was legally required, according to TIMEC's Permissibly-Self-Insured status, to do ALL she possibly could to facilitate prompt medical treatment for me, and to also ENSURE THAT NO FURTHER HARM came to me as an injured worker whose injury she had ample and due corporate notice and mandated responsibility for monitoring throughout this entire ordeal:

1) Barry Raymos, the Human Resources Director of TIMEC, knew all along that he had already deliberately shredded my written complaint of racial discrimination which was presented first to TIMEC in September of 1994, and before another copy was placed by me into my personnel file on February 7, 1995.

2) Brent Babow, the General Counsel of TIMEC knew all along that false and contradictory statements were being compiled and presented as official TIMEC corporate Statements of Position in NLRB and EEOC inquiries, and to their medical-defense expert, psychiatrist Dr. Donald Standford M.D., and

3) that some co-worker in the TIMEC Corporation Administrative Office building the three of them shared, while and during the course of realizing and acknowledging among themselves that I was already clearly suffering with, and showing the symptoms of, job-related psychological and emotional stress due to racial discrimination, made the cold-hearted decision on February 7, 1995, to sneak-attack and further provoke my ailment of anxiety by contacting the EDD and deliberately lying about the circumstances surrounding my lay-off of January 19, 1995, just for the purpose of getting me unjustly sanctioned as a punitive measure.

The professional playbook which TIMEC Risk Management Administrator Sue Evans was legally committed to follow for the implementation of TIMEC's PSI designation and status can be found here at the: California Code of Regulations, Title 8, Chapter 4.5. Division of Workers' Compensation, Subchapter 1.5.Injuries, on or after January 1, 1990....

§10109. Duty to Conduct Investigation; Duty of Good Faith

a) To comply with the time requirements of the Labor Code and the Administrative Director's regulations, a claims administrator must conduct a reasonable and timely investigation upon receiving notice or knowledge of an injury or claim for a workers' compensation benefit.

b) A reasonable investigation must attempt to obtain the information needed to determine and timely provide each benefit, if any, which may be due the employee.

1) The administrator may not restrict its investigation to preparing objections or defenses to a claim, but must fully and fairly gather the pertinent information, whether that information requires or excuses benefit payment. The investigation must supply the information needed to provide timely benefits and to document for audit the administrator's basis for its claims decisions. The claimant's burden of proof before the Appeal Board does not excuse the administrator's duty to investigate the claim.

2) The claims administrator may not restrict its investigation to the specific benefit claimed if the nature of the claim suggests that other benefits might also be due.

e) The duty to investigate requires further investigation if the claims administrator receives later information, not covered in an earlier investigation, which might affect benefits due.

e) The claims administrator must document in its claim file the investigatory acts undertaken and the information obtained as a result of the investigation. This documentation shall be retained in the claim file and available for audit review.

e) Insurers, self-insured employers and third-party administrators shall deal fairly and in good faith with all claimants, including lien claimant.

Apparently, TIMEC Corporation Workers' Compensation Claims Manager-Risk Administrator Sue Evans only read the preceding and aforementioned statute above for no reason other than to be able to accurately and effectively totally ignore it. Her blatant disregard of this important provision, as the appointed administrator for the PSI bond placed by TIMEC with the State of California, hurts me still to this day. There is no "getting over it" for victims of intentionally racist, psychological brutality; there is only moving through it, and past it, into the present and future, which is what I am doing by writing this book.

Chapter 8

~National Labor Relations Board
Finding In My Favor~

The National Labor Relations Board wasted no time at all in officially finding the TIMEC Corporation in error for having placed TIMEC-Shell Martinez, CA maintenance Supervisor John Allen in a position to serve on the TIMEC employee's union contract negotiating committee on behalf of their International Union of Petroleum and Industrial Workers membership under the leadership of IUPIW president Tom Rincon. For that infraction, TIMEC was required to prominently post a large, town-hall styled notice, at each and every TIMEC Company, Inc., job site for a specific number of (I believe 45) days, DETAILING AND INFORMING ALL WORKERS as to the specifics of what they had done wrong. My name was also prominently listed on the postings as the individual worker who had called them out on it. I no longer had a job with TIMEC, and I certainly was missing my friends and co-workers; however, I also knew that I had absolutely struck a blow against TIMEC, in public, and outside of TIMEC's power and control, where all my co-workers could see and acknowledge, every work day.

There was not going to be any financial payout for the NLRB charge finding against TIMEC, and also, the NLRB also did not address the matter of TIMEC's racial discrimination against me in any manner whatsoever. The EDD's bureaucratic changing of my EDD status from unemployed to disabled however, actually gave me a small bump with about a 27 dollar per week upgrade in payment rate.

On my applicant's side of the 1995 Workers' Compensation dispute, I was tasked with either representing myself pro se, or with finding a Workers' Comp applicant's attorney willing to take on my case, with all its baggage for the meager, state-regulated and limited fee of 12 per cent of what could be negotiated to be acquired on my behalf while, in turn, due to the "zealous defense" legal standard of the litigation industry, the TIMEC Corporation had no restrictions whatsoever as to how much money they could spend on attorneys and doctors to present their corporate-sponsored lies of perjury in the effort of illegally denying my legitimate claim.

After not being able to find an applicant's attorney willing to take on the multitude of issues, along with the recently set higher bar for establishing the injury related to my legal quandary with TIMEC, it soon became clear that for me to be financially compensated for my work-related psychiatric stress injury caused by racial discrimination, I would have to, on my own, file a pro se claim against TIMEC for damages under California Labor Code § 3208.3 with the Workers' Compensation Appeals Board. My Workers' Compensation claim case, filed on March 13, 1995 would be litigated long before any federal EEOC civil rights racial discrimination action could, or would, actually take place.

My claim filing on March 13, 1995, was met with Risk-Management Administrator Sue Evan's immediate assertion that she knew absolutely nothing about my injury, which also immediately resulted in giving the TIMEC Corporation 90 MORE days, or until the middle of June, 1995, to investigate and determine the merits of "the applicant's injury". Mind you that TIMEC-Chevron Superintendent Dave Newman had already acknowledged, in a TIMEC Corporation evidentiary position paper for the EDD, as to having personally observed my stress injury on January 19, 1995. So then, in effect, by Sue Evans' deliberately and simply twisting and ignoring of the Workers' Compensation laws concerning her duty of good faith to me under Title 8 § 10109 of the California Code of Regulations, the TIMEC Corporation was given another time extension of opportunity to further and intentionally compound my emotional distress.

I was certainly blessed to have been in the position of being treated by psychologist Dr. Polonsky throughout this continual onslaught of the TIMEC Corporation's ongoing and intentional infliction of emotional distress upon me. In the interim 90-day waiting period, an unexpectedly powerful and beautiful thing began to occur; I was surprisingly found myself able to be led by Dr. Polonsky comfortably into contemplating the true darkness of professional legal minds, and was soon also able to, without fear, come to sensibly understand my task of navigating the unseemly legal pressures and realities which frighten and discourage most novice legal warriors during their initial encounters with the courts as pro se litigants. You see, through my ongoing therapy sessions with Dr. Polonsky, it became clear to me that with TIMEC's concept of legal ethics being a consistent standing oxymoron, and a vibrant, living reality, that it really couldn't be allowed to matter any longer to the point of further disturbing me. What actually DID matter, at that point of my own dance, was that I had to immediately realize, accept, and understand that for whatever reason, perhaps even for reasons which may have been directly bearing upon the very terms of her employment, TIMEC's Risk-Management Administrator Sue Evans was going to lie and do her absolute best to steadfastly maintain, in the face of direct contradiction, of the Newman letter's true and very real existence, that the first she ever heard of me having a work-related injury was my March 13, 1995 filing of my own Workers' Compensation claim.

There had recently been tragic incidents of workplace violence and homicide in the San Francisco Bay Area during the time frame of TIMEC's over-the-top and relentless provocation of my desire and commitment to remain a law-abiding citizen. San Francisco had suffered the 101 California Street Shootings at a law office in July of 1993; and in April of 1995, a receptionist at the Richmond, California, Housing Authority, after previously threatening to pull a '101 California' if dismissed from work, murdered his supervisor and a co-worker when the dismissal occurred. Even in March of 1998, three months before my June, 1998, federal civil rights trial against TIMEC began, a disgruntled worker at the General Chemical plant, right across the street from Dave Newman at TIMEC-Chevron, upset after returning to work from what he felt was an unjust one-week suspension, gunned down two supervisors before taking his own life. In the event I had not reached out for understanding from Jehovah God, and also reached for the psychotherapy which came to be, in my case, a proven medical science which provided me with the necessary tools of reasoning, which enabled me to proceed on my own towards finding a just remedy, the purely evil and insidious nature of the racism proffered by the TIMEC Corporation might have won a significant battle. From TIMEC's fiduciary perspective of counting money and time, if they could have somehow pushed me, or compelled me, to forego the appropriate societal principles of sublimating rage which I was learning to utilize with Dr. Polonsky, they, retrospectively, could have saved a great deal of costs in litigation expenses. The fiduciary reality faced by many corporations, is that the compensation costs for the families of unfortunate victims of workplace violence runs much less than the litigation costs for a full-blown state-and-federal court civil rights jury trial defense. That is, sadly, another cold, hard, legal, fiscal reality fact.

As I earlier stated, the TIMEC Corporation chose Workers' Compensation defense attorney, Carlton H.A. Taber, Esq., of the Oakland, CA law firm of Schmitt, Morris, Bittner & Schmitt to defend themselves against my California Labor Code § 3208.3 psychiatric injury claim. My opinion of attorney Carl Taber's world view soon became one which revealed that he perceived and felt that bullying people was okay and should generally be permitted, providing that the bully was thorough and skilled enough at the techniques of oppression to stultify, or paralyze, their victim into a numb state of perpetual intellectual and emotional inaction in so far as their own self-interests and well-being were concerned.

While I was researching his legal career at the law library, I found that while attorney Taber was a student at the local University of California Hastings College of the Law, he had written an article for the school's Hastings Law Review supporting the position of a man who was accused of emotional spousal abusive battery. Future attorney Carl Taber's position seemed to be, that if the wife could not muster and find the emotional fortitude to, of her own volition, complain to the authorities on her own behalf, about her husband's penchant for, apparently against her wishes, offering his wife's fellatio skills to infrequent guests in their home, the husband was then and absolutely not guilty of anything at all whatsoever. This is the individual attorney which the TIMEC Corporation selected to defend their deliberative actions which injured me at work.

TIMEC's legal defense position to my injury was the affirmative defense provision of California Labor Code 3208.3 (n), which held that if I had not actually been injured by any actual events of racial discrimination; and if my injury, if there actually WAS an "injury", was substantially caused by lawful, nondiscriminatory, good faith personnel actions, then TIMEC was not liable for any aspect of my emotional stress injury, whatsoever. The evidentiary burden of proof for that affirmative defense however, was placed upon TIMEC. So now, instead of my having to prove that I was injured by their actions, THEY then were tasked to prove that the personnel actions which I was complaining about were "lawful, nondiscriminatory and made in good faith".

The medical-legal defense evidentiary aspect of my Workers' Compensation claim was then brought to hinge upon the clinical term referred to as "actual events criteria" by TIMEC's medical-legal expert, psychiatrist Donald H. Standford, MD. In forming his medical diagnosis of my injury, Dr. Standford allegedly began by reviewing an evidentiary package of official TIMEC Corporation position statements which had been presented to various California State and United States federal entities under the authorship of TIMEC Corporation General Counsel Brent Babow. All these aforementioned position statements were subsequently noted by U.S. District Court Judge Susan Illston, during the 1998 federal civil rights trial of John Bumphus vs. TIMEC, C95-3400 (7/10/98), to be deliberately false and misleading; yet, in 1995, psychiatrist Dr. Standford actually considered them to be credible medical evidence towards his determination of my psychological health and emotional bearing.

My belief upon reflection, however, is that most sixth grade elementary school students could have made a more accurate comparison of the time sheet facts contrasted to the statements drawn up by attorney Babow, and then gone to very easily determine that Dr. Standford was only more than eagerly determined to trash and malign his own medical-expert credibility as a practicing psychiatrist, for the legal benefit of the TIMEC Corporation interests in this matter.

My thereto ongoing 1995 quest of using the Law Library to research and find employment law attorneys willing to represent my legal issues, and take my Workers' Compensation and EEOC cases against the TIMEC corporation to court on a contingency, "get paid if you win" basis, was becoming more and more difficult day by day. The lawyers I were initially approaching in the San Francisco Bay Area at that time concerning both legal matters were very professionally polite, yet at the same time very clear and abrupt, in rightly and professionally expressing to me that their time was a very valuable commodity. Oftentimes I would enter law offices for a prospective case-taking 'interview', only to become shortly thereafter frustrated by attorney after attorney who seemingly desired to intellectually shut me down, and overtake my own perception of my litigation. These occurrences made me realize, again and again, after each and every such encounter, that I was NOT an attorney; and the reality of my not being a lawyer while representing myself in legal matters was dangerously short-sighted, and left me remaining dependent upon every trained legal professional's capacity to perceive and explain for me the intricate aspects of complicated legal issues; yet, the recurring blessing which always remained was that I also always, through God's Grace, was able to remember that I wasn't stupid. I was, simply, uneducated in matters of litigation.

Because I had no money for a retainer fee, I would also have to find someone altruistic enough in their legally trained capacity to spend their time fathoming through my whining and rambling ranting about my being mistreated by the TIMEC Corporation. All I had available to offer for such a legal helping hand on behalf of myself was the big pile of "documentation, documentation and documentation" collection pertaining to my every legal interaction with TIMEC, a collection habit which had actually been suggested by the TIMEC Corporation during their "Legal Issues for Supervisors" seminar, and which I in turn had also supplemented with rudimentary legal work and research done on my own behalf. My English reading and writing composition skills were pretty good; however, I was not delusional in that I clearly knew my actual understanding of "legalese" or lawyer-speak, was vocabulary-wise at about a second grader's level. I was absolutely quite certain, with a somewhat sickening sense of impending doom, that without reputable legal representation standing somewhere in the big picture on my behalf, TIMEC's California Bar-card carrying, legal hired-gun attorneys would confuse me totally and completely succeed at shutting all my efforts at remedy out and down entirely and forever, without even giving me the professional courtesy of laughing in my face.

However, along with my new-found educational endeavor of fervently and wholeheartedly learning about the law, and about the history of the law during that time, I was also simultaneously immersed in an equally new personal religious study with a member of my local Fairfield CA., Jehovah's Witness congregation. I was not attending any of their congregational meetings at all; yet, this man, John Duncan, would faithfully come by my apartment every Sunday after his meeting and spend many hours discussing with me, using his vast library of spiritual texts and concordances, how the Bible truths could be applied to not only the furtherance of my life, but also to the spiritual understanding of my legal situation. I was led by him to the instruction by scripture that there were various Biblical incidents of individuals being sent to death by the corrupt and viciously vindictive court system which was intent upon taking their very lives, and that for instance, Jesus' trial was held on the Sabbath Day, when the court was supposed to be closed. I was also impressed with the success of the Jehovah's Witness Organization's lawyers regarding United States Supreme Court litigations pertaining to their right to preach door-to-door. Those realizations, along with their truly international, racial and ethnic-culturally diverse membership really allowed me to listen to what was being said. I merged strongly with the scriptural fact found in the book of Luke which told that it was after Jesus put the lawyers on notice that He had perceived the games that they generally played with the revelation of true scriptural legal knowledge, that it was then when they decided to lay in wait so as to trap Him into the injustice of their wicked court, with His own words. It was already demonstrably clear to me, after what I had been encountering with them thus far, that the TIMEC Corporation was absolutely intent upon perverting justice in their dealings with me; what worried me, and what I urgently needed to discover, was which avenues they may have already officially corrupted.

Chapter 9

~Walnut Creek, CA,
Workers' Compensation Appeals Board~

I had learned, that in order to establish my Workers' Compensation injury under California Labor Code § 3208.3, I would have to first formally file a request for that documentation in a Motion for Discovery, so as to legally compel the TIMEC Corporation to release evidentiary copies of the TIMEC Shell-Martinez work and time-keeping records for September and October of 1994. This request for documentation is legally known as a subpoena duces tecum. I was soon to discover that I was extremely naïve and unknowing, about the level of retaliatory litigation intensity I would spark, by taking my hand-typed subpoena duces tecum request papers to the TIMEC Corporation office in Vallejo. I had innocently supposed and surmised that, after all, facts are facts; and because the proof of the truth of the matter in dispute clearly was known by all to be located in TIMEC's possession, and within the documentation they surely held in their corporate office, that they just therefore knew they would have to 'give it up', because I had already just established that I was now 'clever' enough to put my request on paper in an 'official', actual, Workers' Compensation court matter.

So when they answered my documentation Discovery Motion by filing a Motion to Quash my request, I had no idea in the world how, or why, they thought it could possibly be accepted in court, for them not to produce in court, evidence which established proof of the truth pertaining to the actual core of our dispute concerning the charge of racial discrimination I had claimed against them. On the day of the first Workers' Compensation Appeals Board court hearing, which had been set to get a ruling from the judge on TIMEC's Motion to Quash my pro se subpoena duces tecum requests for documentation, TIMEC attorney Carlton H. A. Taber immediately and abruptly began argument in the hearing by distracting the issue of the evidentiary documentation with an insidiously brilliant and blatant, tricky legal "stunt" maneuver. He calmly, and suddenly, directly told the court an absolute lie with such ease which was, in turn, a lie of such presumptuous magnitude, that I truly had to focus and catch myself from leaning over and smashing him right in the middle of his smugly smirking face. This idiot person, Taber, whom I had never met, or never even heard from, or of, at any point before in my life, was morphing into a 'monster' before my very eyes, as he falsely and directly asserted on the Court record, before Judge Mason, whom I was also meeting for the very first time, that he had been vigorously attempting to contact me in order to take my deposition, but that I had been effectively avoiding him.

I was shocked, stunned, and again completely stultified, right there in my tracks before the judge; I knew that I had never received any contact from attorney Taber, whatsoever. My telephone contact number for all things concerning the TIMEC Corporation was, throughout the entirety of my association with TIMEC, at the home phone land line of my retired parents. Simply put, Taber never called there; I had NEVER missed ANY call having anything to do with TIMEC business. Carl Taber had lied openly in court just to establish to me from the outset that he could, and would, lie whenever he took a notion to do so. I was incapable of focusing on any other matter throughout the brief hearing, because I was subconsciously flinching while paying very close attention to Taber's every word, in an effort to anticipate what kind of false statement he would next make. My duces tecum requests for the much-needed TIMEC Corporation documentation were subsquently summarily quashed and denied, for being insufficient and incomplete in their preparation before the Court. Quashed; (I had always thought the word was "squashed"). More thoughts of incompetent insecurity pertaining to my capacity to legally represent myself flooded into my subconscious reality. I knew that I had done the very best I could to follow what I thought I understood to be the applicable rules of court in my request for the paper yet, due to a "legal technicality", of my own procedural incompetence, and now, because of the monster, Carl Taber. I was denied access to the paperwork which I believed was essential to establishing my prima facie case.

Yes, the California State Legislature had absolutely provided me with a great opportunity by allowing me to represent myself in the Workers' Compensation Appeals Board court proceeding before Judge Mason; however, I soon thereby realized that I was still required to learn and properly apply the rules of that particular court. I quickly came to know that each court, or each and every employment law beaurocracy, had a different set of procedural policies, practices and rules. I, in my anger and rage against the TIMEC Corporation, had filed charges seeking remedy in every forum I could discover. Therefore, EDD, NLRB, California Fair Housing and Employment, EEOC, Workers' Compensation litigations were all open, and waiting to be worked. I absolutely had no other option available whatsoever, but to continue forging forward and ahead, by spending my mornings through evenings at the Law library, reading everything I could about every forum with which I had sought remedy.

Our Workers' Compensation Appeals Board (WCAB), judge and trier of fact, the Honorable George W. Mason, Jr., had received his Juris Doctorate degree from the University of California (Boalt Hall) in 1969. While fortunately, in my opinion, my peace of mind was comfortably affected by the fact that Judge Mason is an African American male, which allowed me the opportunity of presenting my claim based on racial discrimination to someone who knew that racial discrimination actually existed, it was also made very clear to me, from the outset, that my pro se legal activities would now be, without any special court favor, held to a strictly enforced standard level of competence and performance insofar as observing the actual Rules of Court was concerned.

I had to compose and prepare myself, to make certain that the monster Carl Taber's introductory lie would be the only one which would effectively go unchallenged. There would be no 'ex parte' communications, behind each other's back to Judge Mason; and although I was arguing to establish that I had suffered the Infliction of Emotional Distress at the hands of the TIMEC Corporation, it was also immediately apparently clear that any emotional outbursts would most certainly NOT weigh in my favor. My emotions had no place in my own pro se Workers' Comp litigation during hearings; all facts and arguments were to be presented before the Court, coldly and impersonally. I would not be allowed to show anger or fear, or physically attack the monster. I had to fight the war with actual words. That's what 'lawyers' do.

One thing having my Workers' Compensation subpoenas quashed immediately taught me was, that the task of representing myself, and thereby being responsible for the actual presentations of documentation for the litigation of the legal issues required in the establishment of my claims, also required my adherence to a very specific and precise formatting procedure, even as a pro se litigant. I therefore began to glean from, so as to emulate, the copy and style format and phrasings of every legal document I was able to review from any source, and in particular those directed towards me, and my case, by my main legal adversary, who at that time, was attorney Carleton H. A. Taber, esq.

TIMEC Corporation General Counsel attorney Brent Babow was now fading into the background and away from my personal legal conflict battleground; at least as far back as he could stand, from the legal defense litigation mess he had created to that point for TIMEC with his varying degrees of employment law situational incompetence. In my rating-and-ranking-of-lawyers opinion, General Counsel Babow was now no longer viewed by me as a legal soldier, or warrior; he was diminished, in my reality, to being no more than just a legal cheater, an employment law legal industry sub-species, basing, developing and crafting his behind-the-scenes legal reputation as a bully in the workplace, upon his capacity to block and officially obfuscate actual truth and reality into confusing distortions against all the TIMEC employees who were not even inclined to fight him back.

Now, just like a petulant and cowed schoolyard bully, shocked, overwhelmed and reeling at having encountered his first actual bloody lip, which was delivered to his desk by the National Labor Relations Board, he shrank. I was therefore and then officially now dealing directly with the overtly duplicitous attorney monster Taber, the TIMEC Corporation legal "hired gun", whose mission was to come in and "clean up", for them, the Workers' Compensation mess created by TIMEC's workplace legal malevolence.

Chapter 10

~Book of Joshua – Chapter 8~

The Old Testament Book of Joshua opens its 8th Chapter with the phrase, "Then Jehovah said to Joshua: 'Do not be afraid or be terrified'." The Biblical fact of the matter is that sometimes Our Creator directly implores particular individuals to stand firm when approaching what He has Chosen and put on His Schedule as a Great Battle for His Glory. Dr. Polonsky also counseled me by saying, "Do your best, and don't worry…sometimes David actually defeats Goliath".

The Nolo Press section of the law library, which specialized in do-it-yourself primers on legal issues, had a book on Workers' Compensation which was valuable in helping me to understand what I was up against insofar as dealing pragmatically and with a professional's perspective towards the direct legal issues of the Workers' Comp system. In addition, West Publishing had created a "Nutshell" series of legal books which also condensed legal employment law issues into a somewhat more understandable overview.

While I had been compiling my hand-written notes on legal pads, and in lined notebooks, I always realized that at some point, total access to a typewriter was going to be necessary for me to maintain the pace of legal documentation preparation required in my task. I had learned to type during Mrs. Max's early-morning, before-school-started class at Vallejo Junior High in 1968, on one of those big clackity-clack Underwood machines which insisted that I actually depress the key in order to make the symbol arm come up and strike the mechanically-placed ink typewriter ribbon. Suddenly, while I was under this pressure in 1995, a close friend blessed me with a lite-touch 'Brother' brand electric typewriter, which would actually "ding" whenever I misspelled a word. As I began to polish up my 8th grade early morning typing skills, I started on my quest to learn formatting, so as to attempt to create legal documents which could almost somewhat begin to look like everyone else's. The electric typewriter had a flow which made me feel as if I could type and create almost as fast as I could think.

Carl Taber's law office at Schmitt, Morris, Bittner, & Schmitt was located in a conservative bastion section of Oakland, CA, known as "Old Town". After realizing that the monster Taber had a penchant for misrepresenting every required occurrence of interaction between us, I made it a point to hand-deliver all correspondence directly to his office, while insisting upon a signature acknowledgement from a representative in his office upon each delivery. The deposition of me he desired was still looming before the September, 1995 trial date, as was the scheduling of TIMEC's Workers' Compensation defense case mental-health examination, which was to be held at the office of their psychological mental health expert, psychiatrist Dr. Donald Standford, MD, in Berkeley CA. I was required, by Workers' Compensation law, to make myself available, in a timely manner before trial, for both of these TIMEC Corporation requests to acquire first-hand professional perception and assessment of my status and symptoms as a person suffering from the psychological injury which they had already deliberately conspired to cause and compound.

I had never been deposed before. I also knew, and accepted that psychiatrist Dr. Standford could not professionally negate, disprove or dispel the medical reality, or validity, of my treatment sessions with Dr. Polonsky, so I felt that I was balanced and okay in so far as being able to establish the credible evidence of my injury from a medical-legal perspective. However, I also knew that defense attorney Carl Taber was a liar, and a trickster who desperately yearned to use my deposition to destroy my Workers' Comp claim; and I still had not yet been able to secure even a working relationship with any attorney at all, whatsoever, on my behalf.

After receiving my Notice of Right to Sue from the EEOC in Oakland, CA, I was making phone calls to various civil rights attorneys in the East Bay Area, hoping to find someone willing to represent me in federal court on a contingency-fee basis. I was telling each one of them my often-by-then repeated story about me, TIMEC and all the agencies I had filed with for remedy, when suddenly, one of the African American attorneys I had called gave to me, free of charge, the best bit of legal advice I would ever receive. He said, "Call Pamela Price. She's very busy, but if you can get her to represent you, I think you'll be all right." The way he laughingly said it, made me believe that he knew exactly what he was talking about.

I called the office of attorney Pamela Price in Oakland, CA, and asked to speak with "Ms. Price". I was clearly exhausted; one psychologically tired, battle-weary individual. By that point in time, I had already arrived at the notion, as a means of self-defense, of viewing ALL attorneys with a sense of cautious skepticism and dread. They were, after all, the masters of a craft wherein a simple slip in the turning of a phrase, could immediately bring either victory, or defeat. A good practitioner of law has been trained to dominate every legal conversation they're ever in. I was not a good practitioner of law; I was an angry black man with an orphan civil rights racial discrimination case. The Notice of Right to Sue I had received from the EEOC was only my ticket to the party, and certainly not redeemable for an automatic seat at the table.

The legal assistant lady who had answered my phone call had a very pleasant voice, and as she let me know that Ms. Price was not available to speak with me at that moment, she also seemed very interested in hearing everything I had to say about my situation with the TIMEC Corporation. I seized the opportunity to talk, talk and talk; and surprisingly, her only interruptions were to make sure that I was telling my full and complete story, all about TIMEC, Shell-Martinez, Chevron, Dave Newman, the NLRB, the EDD, Workers' Compensation, my California Department of Fair Employment and Housing (DFEH) filing, my EEOC filing, Dr. Polonsky, and Carl Taber-everything, to the best of my understanding. She then told me that she would inform Ms. Price that I had called, and would tell her what I had communicated to her about my situation. I immediately felt better, as I had been longing for quite some time to tell my full and complete legal story to someone in the legal profession who was not immediately trying to run a game on me.

The same lady called me the next day so as to schedule a meeting for me with Ms. Price. I arrived early for the appointment, and had brought along with me every document I had in my possession pertaining to anything I had ever been litigating with the TIMEC Corporation. I was ushered into a large conference room to await Ms. Price's arrival. While I was waiting, I was making mental notes: "Stay calm, speak clearly, maintain eye contact, be a respectful potential client." Ms. Price entered the conference room with a calming presence which immediately put me at ease; her professional bearing impacted our introduction, and I could feel her looking right through me as we began to speak about my dilemma. After our discussion, as she shared with me the reality and logistics of her very busy schedule, she let me know that she would see what kind of time she actually had available to deal with my situation, and let me know. She then assured me, that if she couldn't personally take my case, she would find someone who would. I was elated and 'over the moon' with anticipation. A 'real lawyer', an African American woman who had her own law firm, with her own very busy law office, had actually spoken to the validity of my civil rights claim of racial discrimination against the TIMEC Corporation. My orphan case was an orphan no longer.

Chapter 11

~And Ya' Don't Stop~

I didn't know anything at all about attorney Pamela Y. Price before I first stepped into her office in 1995. All the research I had done on all the previous lawyers I had contacted was based on information I found in the big "Martindale-Hubble" books in the law library directory listing of licensed attorneys. The Martindale Hubble listings show information such as an attorney's educational background, and association affiliations. Ms. Price's main credential, as far as I was concerned, was framed under glass on her wall, in the waiting-room lobby of her office. It was a news article about the 1994 case of former San Quentin prison sergeant Lisa D. Pulido, who had been sexually harassed to the point of being driven away from her job by unwanted advances while the California Department of Corrections looked the other way. Ms. Price had argued before, and convinced, a Marin County Superior Court judge that the 41-year-old Ms. Pulido had been subjected to a hostile work environment and was entitled to compensation for lost wages and emotional distress; the judge then went on to award Ms. Pulido a $1.3 million dollar judgment. That was all I needed to know; this attorney is a winner, and I was in desperate need of a win against the TIMEC Corporation. My ex-Brother-in-law, William McMullen, had been a lieutenant at San Quentin during the time of the Pulido trial. When stopped by to visit him at his home in Vallejo, to tell him about the conversation that I had with Ms. Price, and about my quest to find an attorney to help me deal with TIMEC. He also, just like the attorney who first recommended Pam Price, let me know that as far as he could tell, she would be the absolute best attorney I could possibly ever find. When I mentioned the Pulido trial and judgment verdict, he said, "Yeah. I got called in to testify at the trial in that case. She's very good at what she does, Man…and I'll tell you something else; I NEVER want to be on the other side against her in a courtroom again."

Attorney Pam Price's representative called me in for another meeting whereby Ms. Price again made my day, by agreeing to represent me in my federal civil rights litigation against the TIMEC Corporation.

As I listened attentively so as to learn about the terms in our now attorney/client contractual relationship, I found myself still tense and nervous, and somewhat trembling with anxiety. I was very carefully measuring my words, as I was also doing my very best to sincerely communicate my gratitude, as I provided her with whatever, and all other, pertinent information she sought about my situation. Suddenly there, right then, while sitting in her office, I gradually began to feel the emergence of a safe hedge of protection from all the legal bullying I had endured; bullying which had been storming, swarming, battering and surrounding me, all around, ongoing, and for months. I really didn't want to mess this opportunity up by shooting myself in the foot with my own mouth. All that nervousness immediately cleared up when she simply and smilingly said to me, "From now on, just call me Pam." I sighed and exhaled with relaxed laughter; it was all good.

As a novice in the world of major-league civil rights litigation, I had no idea whatsoever about what to expect from the TIMEC Corporation insofar as their legal defense representation for my case. I realized pretty well early on that they already knew their Workers' Compensation defense attorney, Carl Taber, could never match wits with Pam Price. No, for their federal civil rights litigation defense, the TIMEC Corporation reached out and tapped the law firm of Littler, Fastiff, Tischy, Mendelson & Mathiason, P.C., which was the largest labor law defense firm in America. Littler-Mendelson, at that time, according to the Martindale-Hubble guide, had 16 offices nationwide, and a battalion of over 200 lawyer associates. Pam Price, in turn, did not want anything at all to do with my Workers' Compensation case; therefore it then totally became my responsibility to deal with Carl Taber, on my own and to the best of my ability, win or lose.

My desire, as a federal civil rights litigation client, was to not only sue TIMEC as a corporation, but to also sue as many TIMEC Corporation Supervisory personnel individually and out of their own personal pockets as was possible; Pamela Price, as my legal representative, appropriately laid that hot stack of pressure right on top of the heads of five TIMEC supervisory employees. Federal Discovery in preparation for the civil trial was now coming, and the subpoenas duces tecum which were now being prepared by the office of my very real and accomplished attorney, instead of haphazardly by myself, were not in any danger at all of being quashed by the federal court for technical inconsistency in their preparation. Also now, the onerous, ominous, dread of facing a deposition was no longer my concern alone and in isolation; because along with the TIMEC Five defendants, quite a few other TIMEC Corporation employees were being notified by federal subpoena that they were now required, by law, to sit for depositions in this matter.

With the guidance and assistance of the professional attorneys in Pam Price's office, I was able to learn and discuss how to speak my truth into the defendant's record while protecting my interests from being scrambled by their lawyers during my required depositions. Shortly thereafter, during my own Workers' Compensation deposition, I immediately discovered, from the outset, that I had been correct in anticipating Carl Taber's pressing desire to harm the core of my racial discrimination argument by tricking me into testifying against myself. I did not have the funds available, as an injured worker and pro se applicant litigant, to hire a court recording transcriber in order to allow me the opportunity to depose the TIMEC Corporation supervisory personnel before trial; therefore, at our Workers' Compensation trial, I would be hard-pressed and required to get them to talk on the official court record as much as possible, because now, with their being at risk of having to pay personally for damages in my federal civil litigation, their self-serving and self-protecting statements under oath suddenly were running the risk, on the record, of being revealed to be clearly in direct conflict with each other. In addition, my plan of purchasing a copy of the actual Workers' Compensation trial court transcript, for my own personal purview, was more affordable, and within my very meager and tight legal budget.

On the other hand, my attorney Pam Price, and her associates, had the resources to depose everyone and anyone who may have had a story to tell pertaining to my federal civil rights racial discrimination litigation, It was oftentimes hilarious, and yet sometimes alternately infuriating during their depositions, to observe from my team's perspective, the "other side" of litigation ass-whipping, while the TIMEC Corporation supervisory and administrative personnel squirmed and attempted to manufacture lies out of thin air, as their hired team of Littler-Mendelson defense attorneys were doing their absolute professional best, to protect them from themselves, as they repeatedly made contradictory statements under oath, knowing that they were also ultimately testifying for the actual federal court record under penalty of perjury.

After the completion of the September, 1995 Workers' Compensation trial, all I could do productively was impatiently wait for Judge Mason's finding of fact, while continuing to behave in a manner so as not to cause any complications in my federal civil rights trial. I began to read up on the legal antics and tactics perpetrated by the Littler-Mendelson Firm in behest of defending their clients. They were, clearly, a "no holds barred" group of litigators. However in the instance of my personal litigation, unlike the script set by Brent Babow and Carl Taber they, for the most part, seemed to work very hard at playing strictly within the rules. The contrast was often startling and yes, once again, somewhat psychologically intimidating; but this time, along with having Dr. Polonsky counseling and guiding me, I was blessed with Pam Price as my attorney. The actual odds were something like 200-to-3, attorney-wise, in Littler's favor, yet Pam NEVER flinched, not one time. I was painstakingly and thoroughly prepared by Pam Price's office for the three arduous deposition sessions which Littler-Mendelson insisted upon putting me through at their big, luxurious, 20th floor, panoramic-view office suites in San Franciso.

In April of 1996 Pam and I went to a mandated settlement conference for the case at the San Francisco law office of a firm which was actually named "Low, Ball & Lynch". My instinctive immaturity over the irony of the firm name kept me chuckling inside like a silly kid, all day long; I absolutely saw it as an ominous sign, and I just knew that we weren't going to arrive at a settlement on that day. However, something perceptible and remarkable happened with me and my attorney on our walk-and-talk laugh session while going back to the San Francisco BART station from the settlement conference. For some reason during our informal conversation, it became clear to me that my attorney suddenly realized that EVERYTHING I had been telling her pertaining to the evidence in my case was the absolute truth. And that this fact had now given her an advantage I couldn't quite yet perceive, but was indeed one which I felt she would certainly utilize to its fullest advantage.

The decision made in WCK0023185 by Workers' Compensation Appeals Board Walnut Creek CA, Presiding Judge George W. Mason Jr.'s Finding of Fact, was that I had suffered a Cumulative Stress Injury to my psyche, which was caused by my employment with the TIMEC Corporation. TIMEC defense attorney Carlton Taber had argued, while putting forth the affirmative defense provision of Labor Code § 3208.3 (n), that because TIMEC-Shell Supervisor John Allen, and Rodney Barbush, the white TIMEC-Shell maintenance employee who was given my overtime opportunity rode to-and-from work together in a car pooling situation, it was then only "sensible" and indeed a non-discriminatory job action, to let Barbush work the extra hours, because "he was going to have to wait" on John Allen to conclude supervising the overtime, anyway. My counter to that argument was based on the United States Supreme Court ruling in the 1971 case of *Griggs vs Duke Power Co.*, 401 U.S. 424 (1971), which let me point out that as an employer, TIMEC was required to prove a "business necessity" for an incident which caused a racially disparate impact to me. The overarching fact was that I was not a participant in, or beneficiary of, the car-pooling arrangement between Rodney Barbush and the TIMEC-Shell Supervisor, John Allen; therefore, I argued, the car-pooling should not be considered in argument to be a legitimate TIMEC Company "business necessity". Thus, the illicit taking of my two-and-one-half hours of overtime was indeed discriminatory and non-sensible.

Carl Taber immediately filed a Petition for Reconsideration to appeal Judge Mason's finding with the California State Workers' Compensation Appeals Board in San Francisco. Well, okay Carl. I, in turn, also had two aspects of Judge Mason's ruling for which I sincerely felt I should have been awarded a supplemental compensation: 1.) the Labor Code §132a sanction for discriminating against injured workers, and 2.) the Labor Code §4553 sanction for Serious and Wilful Misconduct by the actions on the part of an executive, managing officer, or general superintendent thereof the TIMEC Corporation. And when I saw the number 4 on the list of grounds for reasoning which could be applied for Reconsideration:

("4. Petitioner has discovered new evidence material to him which he could not with reasonable diligence have discovered and produced at the hearing.") I became, actually and in fact, ecstatic. The federal case depositions of TIMEC Corporation supervisory and administrative personnel sworn under oath and taken by Pam Price & Associates clearly and prominently displayed instance upon instance of illegal duplicity, malfeasance and general wrongdoing which had been perpetrated against me, due to my complaining about racial discrimination and maltreatment. It was overwhelmingly, in my pro se layperson's opinion, a virtual motherload of an evidentiary avalanche. The confused lies, "lapses of memory", and cross-firing misstatements of Barry Raymos, Dave Newman, John Allen and Geno Kitsch during their federal civil trial depositions were all recorded and coded in published, titled volumes, under oath, by the professionally Certified Court Recorder. I cherry-picked from their now-certified conflicting statements, which I clearly could not have been able, with all due diligence, to have discovered and produced for the Workers' Compensation trial back in September of 1995, to establish my now-fresh argument that truly, the Labor Code section §132a and §4553 sanctions should most certainly apply in my favor.

There was also the matter of the cascading penalty aspect of the California Labor Code § 5814 violations committed by the TIMEC Company for not paying my medical providers in a timely manner. I had been seeing Dr. Polonsky, in addition to Chiropractor Dr. Winston Boler for quite some time as TIMEC Claims Administrator Sue Evans steadfastly refused to pay anything at all towards my medical costs. Carl Taber and Sue Evans were holding on, during their Petition for Reconsideration, to the theme set by their psychiatric expert Dr. Standford's opinion, that the "actual events criteria" pertaining to whether, or not, I had been racially discriminated against was not, based on the documentary evidence provided to him by the TIMEC Company, conclusive enough for him to agree with my assertion that I had indeed been.

It had been no matter to Dr. Standford's diagnosis of me that the TIMEC Company had actually been placed on official notice by the California EDD for making a false statement pertaining to my Unemployment Insurance Benefits, or that the National Labor

Relations Board had actually decided in ruling that TIMEC had been found, based upon my having filed a complaint, to have acted improperly by placing TIMEC-Shell Supervisor John Allen on the IUPIW employee's contract negotiating committee, or even that an EDD Independent Medical Examiner (IME) psychologist, Dr, Achamalla, had found in diagnosis that I was suffering work-related stress caused by racial discrimination; and that ALL these "actual events" occurred BEFORE he received his "magic packet" of documents authored by General Counsel Brent Babow, and provided by Carl Taber at the behest of Sue Evans.

The statute of California Labor Code § 5814.(a) reads: "When payment of compensation has been unreasonably delayed or refused, either prior to or subsequent to the issuance of an award, the amount of the payment unreasonably delayed or refused shall be increased up to 25 percent or up to ten thousand dollars ($10,000), whichever is less." So by rights, along with owing me personally a 50 percent bonus addendum for both the 132a and 4553 violations, TIMEC also owed a 25 percent bonus addendum to my medical providers. Of course, I wanted everybody to get PAID. Therefore, I filed my own Petition for Reconsideration to the Workers' Compensation Appeals Board.

Chapter 12

~Waiting It Out~

I had neither quit, nor resigned my job at the TIMEC Corporation; I had, instead, been unlawfully discharged from my employment with TIMEC due to my complaining about racial discrimination. The long and tedious grind of waiting for the wheels of justice to conclusively turn in my favor was eased by the work I began doing in 1996 at the Continentals of Omega Boys & Girls Club, Inc., in Vallejo, CA. I am, actually, one of the six original boys who were chosen by Mr. Philmore Graham to begin the club thirty years earlier, in 1966. In the year of 1966, Philmore Graham was a 27 year-old, newlywed black man who, after graduating with honors from Tennessee State Agricultural & Industrial University before receiving an Honorable Discharge as a Lieutenant in the United States Air force in 1965, had subsequently been hired to direct the Foam Vessels Salvage and Research program at the Mare Island Naval Shipyard in Vallejo. He was also my next-door neighbor, and his parking space at the brand new apartments into which he had just moved, was right across from my Maxwell Alley bedroom window on Shasta St.

I was twelve years old in 1966. In our neighborhood, and at that time in life as young black boys, "running the streets" literally meant no more than that we ran most everywhere we went; we ran to play, we ran home from school, and we ran to visit each other's homes. We were running a Shasta St. game of three-on-three two-hand-touch football in front of "Mr. Phil's" apartment one November evening when he was arriving home from work. After parking his car, he stepped up, still in his shirt-and-tie, and watched our dueling air show. During a break in play he said, "Let me see that ball, Man.". I kind of soft tossed it, easy-like to him, politely and such. He smirked and said, "I thought you could really throw, Man, what was THAT?" I laughed and said, "All right, throw it back. I'll show you some fire." Just that easily, he had captured our full and total attention.

From that initial encounter, we formed the original "Continental's" boy's club, which quickly grew to encompass the block, the neighborhood, the local Friendship Baptist Church, and the entire black community of Vallejo, California, and even expanding in its outreach theme throughout the Bay Area on into San Franciso, CA, as the Omega Boys Club, before locally becoming, after incorporation, the Continentals of Omega Boys & Girls Club, Inc. By 1996, Phil Graham was retired from Mare Island, and yet he was still, as he always had been, devoting more of his personal time than he actually had available in the course of one day to the club. We were all genuinely concerned about his general health and physical well-being; and since I was no longer working with TIMEC, I had the time to fit in and assist him by accompanying him at some of the "show up" endeavors and meetings with club benefactors and associates, and to also remind him to keep on schedule with a much more sensible going home at the end of each day by sometimes nudging him towards the door in the evening at 5:00 p.m. Over the years of our knowing each other, Phil is my family, while still being my mentor. He has always been, was then, and has yet continued to be, the perfect role model as a black man; and while I certainly was not ever the perfect kid, or man, he has remained a consistently supportive friend of mine. It's just been that way, since 1966.

My Boys & Girls Club duties in 1996 evolved into the position of overseeing the implementation of the Club's SMART (Skills Management and Resistance Training) moves program at five after school sites approved by the Vallejo, California, Unified School District. Working with, and for, the children, while watching them grow together as culturally diverse peers, helped to keep me centered by reminding me that there were actually larger concerns than just what I was individually going through with my racial discrimination litigation. Our Vallejo, California, community was struggling to maintain viability within an evaporating economy. Philmore Graham and the Continentals Board of Directors worked tirelessly to keep the doors of the club open with programs for all the children of Vallejo. Many of the boys I grew up with in the club became very successful and prominent professional black men, in the image of men such as Philmore Graham, while many more others, such as myself, were still trying to find our way through life's various mazes, while all along constantly battling the insidious employment schemes of institutionalized and oppressive racism, just to effect some semblance of security within this American Dream.

During the federal case pre-trial preparation, Pam called a few of my co-workers, some of who were actual witnesses to some of the particular instances of TIMEC's ongoing system of racism in the workplace in for deposition, and/or interview,. She also called in and interviewed Philmore Graham. I also sat through and observed while John Allen, Barry Raymos, Dave Newman and Geno Kitsch were deposed by Pam's associate attorneys. I had to learn, very early on, not to react with outbursts of rage while witnessing their attorney-guided efforts at protecting themselves. The weight of the matter was slowly becoming clear to them; these TIMEC supervisors had personally been named as defendants in the federal trial, yet the Littler- Mendelson defense firm was representing them as well, while also defending the TIMEC Corporation, Inc. More and more, the lies and illicit actions perpetrated by these various individual employees were being revealed right before my very eyes and ears, as they inadvertently, and over and over again, told on each other, and told lies, while selfishly trying to personally protect their own self-interests.

The Workers' Compensation Appeals Board Petitions for Reconsideration which had been presented by TIMEC's lawyer Carl Taber, and by myself as a pro se applicant representative, were both denied. According to the Board, Walnut Creek, CA, Presiding Workers' Compensation Judge George W. Mason Jr.'s, finding was accurate and complete. And although I was disappointed in that the Labor Code §132a and § 4553 supplementary sanctions had not been applied against the TIMEC Corporation, I was still very much relieved, and I felt a sense of vindication in having established my injury before the full Workers' Compensation Board. However, and of course, neither TIMEC, nor Carl Taber was finished with me, or with this matter of denying my injury; he immediately served notice that, under the terms of California Labor Code § 5950, he was going to file a Petition for Writ of Review of the Board's decision to the 1st District Court of Appeal in San Francisco.

So then, once again, to protect myself and again represent my interests as a pro se Workers' Compensation injured applicant litigant, I found myself faced with what initially and on the surface appeared to be another overwhelming legal task; now, aside from trying to anticipate what ugly and twisted path the Taber monster was going to take in his Petition for Writ of Review, I was also additionally going to be required to, within a fast-moving 45 days, learn how to prepare my own Petition precisely fitting the organization, publishing and binding format required by the Rules of the Court of Appeal. I went to the 2nd Circuit Court Clerk's office to review, so that I could take notes in order to accurately emulate a properly prepared Petition for Writ of Review. Because, it was also explained to me, that if I were to submit an improperly prepared Petition, it would more than likely result in its being summarily dismissed, without ever having received any review, or acknowledgement, whatsoever.

I was still working my electric type writer, white-out, copies-from-Kinko's system of legal document preparation; Pam Price's team of professional attorneys worked, and thought, with such seemingly effortless lightning-fast word-processing speed and the efficiency provided by the latest technology innovations. I continued to plod along, at my own "turtle's" pace, observing, from outside the circle, how true legal players play the game while, just as she and I had initially discussed and agreed upon from the outset of our agreement, the Workers' Compensation case, pressures, issues, responsibilities and work were still mine alone to bear.

I filed my properly prepared and timely pro se Petition for Writ of Review, on November 2, 1996, with the 1st District Court of Appeal, just as Carl Taber did on behalf of the TIMEC Corporation, and as I did, I also took note of the fact that although I had won my case before Judge Mason, and even though his finding in my favor as an injured worker had met with the approval of the Workers' Compensation Appeals Board, TIMEC still had not yet been required to begin to prepare to deliver not even one penny of payment of my Temporary Disability Payments. My treating doctors were also still awaiting payment for services rendered on my behalf.

Chapter 13

~The Game Gets Flipped~

In April of 1997 I received notice that the 1st District Court of Appeal, after considering the Petitions for Writ of Review, let Judge Mason's original finding of the cumulative stress injury to my psyche stand. The TIMEC Corporation was now required to pay my back Temporary Disability Payments, pay my medical providers, and assist in my Vocational Rehabilitation. Also now, I was required to see a qualified medical evaluator (QME) in order to establish a Permanent Disability Rating, which would determine how much TIMEC would have to pay me for my work-related injury.

I had also found out that although the 1st District Court of Appeal had not chosen to adjust the damages on my claim to meet the Labor Code § 132a and § 4553 penalties, I was still free to Petition the original Workers' Compensation court to re-open my claim for adjustment in these matters, based upon the fraud perpetrated by TIMEC supervisors and administrators which had been uncovered during their sworn depositions which had been taken in preparation for my federal civil action against TIMEC; and of course, that Petition to Reopen is exactly what I, as a pro se litigator, most certainly also immediately did file in April of 1997.

QMEs are physicians licensed to practice in California as medical doctors, such as chiropractors and psychologists, and are certified by the Division of Workers' Compensation Medical Unit to perform medical/legal evaluations. TIMEC had already misspent their medical expert credibility into the hands of psychiatrist Dr. Donald Stanford, MD back in May of 1995, yet defense attorney Carl Taber was now still planning to skewer my Permanent Disability Rating, by illicitly grasping control of the QME process.

Carl Taber's legal meandering had now been reduced to making a scrambling attempt to block the revelation of and explain away, in response to my Petition to Reopen, the plethora of lies and contradictory misstatements made by TIMEC Corporation supervisory and administrative personnel within the original Workers Compensation Court trial transcripts, as they now prominently stood out in blaring contrast, to the previously unavailable yet now newly created and sworn, reviewed, and certified federal trial deposition statements, all made under oath with the Littler defense attorneys sitting with them in Pam Price's office, advising them before a certified court reporter. There was no longer remaining, in my opinion, any hint or rumor of a truthful or honorable avenue of escape available for Carl Taber's reputation as a Workers' Compensation Defense attorney. By failing to eliminate my Workers' Compensation claim in the 1st District Court of Appeal, he was, whether he knew it, or not, done.

I was given a QME panel list of three psychologists from which to choose one to conduct the Qualified Medical Evaluation necessary to resolve the issue of degree of compensable injury I had suffered due to my employment. I chose from the panel a woman doctor, a white female located in Martinez, CA. The QME process involved required that TIMEC, through Carl Taber, must initially and first provide me the documentary materials in their possession which they intended to have the doctor consider during my examination; and in the event I disagreed or disputed the said materials (which had already been proven through federal civil case deposition to be false, and laced with deliberate perjury), I could object to their presentation beforehand, and bring the matter back to be ruled on by Judge Mason. Carl Taber, of course, had no such intention of following this stated and written rule of the Workers' Compensation procedures. So, imagine my lack of amazement when the chosen psychologist contacted me on the day before the scheduled evaluation to inform me that she would not be able to see me and conduct the evaluation, due to the fact that Carl Taber had delivered "an enormous amount" of written materials to her office just three days before I was due in her office, and that there was no way which she could peruse through that much information before meeting with me. And, of course, Taber, again "pretended" to attempt to be following the rule of sharing with me, beforehand, the materials sent to the evaluator, by mailing to me at the same time what amounted to less than one-fifth of the total which he sent to her, totally flaunting the law which directed that I was required to see ALL the selected materials before ANYTHING was presented to the examiner. I was thereby forced to choose another psychologist from the aforementioned QME panel list.

After examining the remaining two names on the panel, I chose the name of Dr. O.S. Glover, in Richmond, CA. I now realize that there have actually occurred times and events during my life, when I've felt spiritually carried along a twisted path while safely resting in the palm of Our Creator's protective hand. My meeting with, and making the acquaintance of the African American male psychologist "Dr. O.G." for my QME examination was, without a doubt, one of those times. Dr. Ira Polansky, Ph D., as my treating psychologist, had absolutely been essential, up to that point in time, to holding my fractured psyche together thus far and throughout the sordid ordeal with TIMEC; however, now the advent of Dr. Glover, just at the prospect of his being a psychologist having had the personal experience of emerging, as a black man, to professional success as a helicopter pilot and law enforcement supervisor in Atlanta, GA, before eventually joining the staff of psychoanalysts at the California State Department of Corrections, into my legal case in order to render his professional opinion on the actual events criteria inherent in this medical-legal dispute, left me comforted in knowing that he would know, and could hear exactly, what I was still somewhat attempting to fully express.

After successfully and illegally destroying my initial choice, and scuttling away my scheduled QME appointment with the Martinez, CA psychologist, Carl Taber now immediately went into having a petulant, whining, diatribe of a hissy fit on paper, while objecting very strenuously and overboard to my selection of Dr, Glover from the remaining two names from the QME panel list I had been sent by the Workers' Compensation Appeals Board. Attorney Taber, on behalf of the TIMEC Corporation, promptly stated, in writing, that he would never pay any bills for services rendered by Dr. Glover. In his complaining papers to the Workers' Compensation Appeals Board concerning this matter, he unprofessionally went so far as to attest officially and in argument on the court record, that the real problem, with the particular Workers' Compensation claim of John Dan Bumphus, Jr., against the TIMEC Corporation, was the fact that myself as the injured applicant, Judge Mason as the sitting trier of fact, and Dr. Glover as the official selected QME panel examiner were all African Americans. Go figure.

While awaiting a ruling from Judge Mason on my Petition to Reopen the Labor Code §§ 132(a) and 4553 components of my Workers' Compensation case, while also going through the process of adjusting to the Vocational Rehabilitation process, I was also anxiously waiting for the actual federal civil rights trial to begin. The federal case Summary Judgment Motions had been filed by TIMEC's Littler defense attorney, resulting in all the personal lawsuits against TIMEC supervisors being dismissed; yet the core of my racial discrimination civil rights case against the TIMEC Corporation still remained. My attorney Pam Price was clearly prepared and ready to do her thing with what we had left. Then, just before the first scheduled trial date, TIMEC Human Resource Director Barry Raymos suffered a heart attack. The trial was going to have to be postponed while he recovered.

During the wait for the federal trial to begin, my Temporary Disability Payments were being issued by the law office of Schmitt, Morris, Bittner & Schmitt, at the direction of Workers' Compensation defense attorney Carleton H. A. Taber. I had initially received a back-payment-owed check from TIMEC after the 1st District Court of Appeal held in my favor by judicially acknowledging the injury to my psyche earlier in the year. Carl Taber was soon and again doing his meddlesome best to irritate what little tranquility I was striving to maintain. My checks were sporadically arriving at irregular intervals, and no one at the Workers' Compensation Appeals Board, or anywhere else, seemed to be able to compel Taber to behave fairly, and according to the prescribed and legal precepts inherent in our interactions. Therefore, and at that time, I seriously contemplated and considered committing a measured, violent act against Carl Taber; not a fatality, or even a severely disabling injurious act, just something which would unalterably bring him, and me, to a mutually agreed understanding. My reasoning was that I felt it was an overwhelmingly established matter of written and public court record that the more I complained about Taber's misdeeds, the wilder and more erratically he proceeded to continue behaving towards and against my interests. I had no criminal record, no felonies whatsoever.

Therefore, I was becoming willing to take my chances in criminal court on being able to prove that, as an individual knowingly suffering from legally established psychological stress, I was being continuously and deliberately provoked in a manner which I could no longer bear. I then called the office of my psychologist, Dr. Ira Polonsky, Ph.D., and discussed my feelings. Subsequently in resolution, no one was hurt, or arrested; and all my Temporary Disability Payment Checks were thereafter promptly delivered, and in good order.

The State of California Department of Industrial Relation's Permission to Self-Insure (PSI) Designation was given to the TIMEC Company Inc., so that they could administer their own injured worker's program. According to the ca.gov website, "The Office of Self Insurance Plans (OSIP) is a program within the director's office of the Department of Industrial Relations (DIR) responsible for the oversight and regulation of workers compensation self-insurance within California. OSIP is also responsible for establishing and insuring that required security deposits are posted by self-insurers in amounts sufficient to collateralize against potential defaults by self-insured employers and groups." In my opinion, particularly after enduring her deliberative and harmful ignorance pertaining to the actual facts and issues relating to my injury, alongside of also enduring the unrelenting abuses which were presented as a legal defense, by her chosen attorney Carl Taber, TIMEC Company Inc. Risk Management Claims Administrator Sue Evans was clearly failing horribly in her state-regulated and corporate-assigned duties to me as an injured worker. Therefore, I filed a Petition with the Workers' Compensation Appeals Board in Walnut Creek, Ca, to revoke the permission of the TIMEC Corporation to self-insure.

END OF PART ONE

EPILOGUE

"WAS THE BATTLE TRULY NECESSARY?"

Now, in 2013, I've found that I was able, in spite and because of my pain, to learn that the concept of "legal ethics" remains, in its existence, as a formidable oxymoron; that finding is due in great part to my acquisition of the knowledge that Ethics, and Finance are, in reality, natural enemies. I would even reach to presume that an attorney with an undergraduate degree in Economics, such as lawyer Brent Babow, would be hard pressed to formulate a credible, critical thinking disagreement to my assertion. The unwritten code governing our American Society currently still dictates that when African Americans are continually and systematically abused on their jobs through means employing tactics based upon racist discriminatory animus, those persecuted black people must continue to learn, accept and ultimately understand that they are obligated to NEVER consider violence as a means of remedying the situation. All that we as black people ever are actually ALLOWED by law and society to do, according to those dictums is complain, and then fervently pray that someone even cares, because no matter how those complaints are served and received, there is no guarantee that "troublemakers" such as myself, will just benignly be left alone to sullenly sulk in the shadows. Fortunately, in my instance, the actual, hand-written complaint I filed with my employer was openly and in private group scoffed at, mocked, and ignored, before it was subsequently forced into the light of day through litigation, before it was thereby found and admitted to have been summarily shredded by the one designated Human Resource Director Administrative person, within the entirety of the TIMEC Corporation, whose absolute and non-negotiable duty of care to me as an employee, required that he see it through to resolution. My life's path has thereby now been unfalteringly changed, forevermore.

I am now, by way of the Social Security Administration, officially designated and acknowledged as a psychologically disabled person due to my experiences as an employee with the TIMEC Corporation. Yes, I am a person who has actually and officially been rendered disabled by racism in the American workplace. I am still in treatment for the post-traumatic emotional stress disorder symptoms purposely inflicted upon me by those within the TIMEC Company, Inc., who sought, and fought wholeheartedly with full malice, to punish me severely for speaking out to them, within their own conflict resolution system, before I ever even considered going to the federal government, about one single, simple occurring act of just one of their racially discriminatory practices. Their retaliatory onslaught of abuses and lies fired and wielded against me for complaining throughout our various litigation procedures has fully and forever provided me with a painful and eternal insight, and a coinciding, clear, perspective towards understanding, as to the full extent which they actually were willing to go to, just to avoid ever be proven in a court of law to be practicing racists, while all along knowing that the sheer multitude of their illicit actions in defending themselves, clearly more than established the point of their deeply-entrenched culture of racism being far beyond any possible chance of disputation.

There are apparently and still today, big and ongoing corporate dollars to be made in the legal protection and litigation defense industry of protecting and covering for racist corporate bigots. The TIMEC Corporation's federal litigation defense firm choice, Littler Mendelson, is still headquartered in San Franciso, Ca, and has now grown from 16 offices to 56 national and global, while their battalion of defense attorneys has in turn grown from 200 to above 900. Workers' Compensation defense attorney Carl Taber, still a member of the California Bar, continues to practice in Petaluma CA. And TIMEC General Counsel Brent Babow who, after using his multidisciplinary legal expertise to help TIMEC grow from $55 Million to over $130 Million in revenue in 9 years, while holding several key positions, including General Counsel, Vice President, and COO, before going on to co-lead a management buy-out of TIMEC founder Briggs Woods, participated in several other acquisitions, and created new divisions, before then being generally responsible for the strategic planning and development of the brand-new TIMEC management team, now leisurely plays in a band on the side.

I have always intended to write this book about my journey in litigation with the TIMEC Corporation; the only issue for me was whether, or not, I would ever be able to sublimate my rage and thoughts effectively enough to chronicle my experiences in a cogent manner. Now I have discovered, after my victories in court against the TIMEC Corporation, that I've also surprisingly attained the unofficial status of absolutely being the ONE runaway slave whom no one really wants to catch. Like so many others before me, I've earned my freedom during my war; and it was earned the hard and direct way, right in the faces of those who would psychologically and emotionally enslave me, by forcing me to accept and cooperate with a corporate reality which holds me to inherently be a lesser person, simply because of the color of my skin.

In November of 2005, while I was living in Phoenix, Arizona, and at home recovering from July, 2005, heart attack surgery due to a ruptured and separated upper aorta, I read the tragic news on the internet, that my original-hero treating psychologist, trusted friend and all-around together wonderful, caring and insightful good-guy human being, Dr. Ira Eugene Polonsky, Ph. D., had been murdered in his office on Capitol St. in Vallejo, CA, by a large man carrying a gun who had entered the office building as one of Dr. Polonsky's clients was preparing to depart after a session. Dr. Polonsky, who had actually been trained in the martial arts, courageously stepped forward, getting to the man, before wrestling with him in the hallway corridor for control of the large weapon, when he then was shot and wounded in his side before subsequently dying there.

Writing these books has been, and certainly shall continue to be, therapeutic; my current mental health professionals have been very helpful in encouraging me to move forward with acknowledging the importance of my telling my true story on paper. My previous writing efforts were all quickly interrupted and derailed by still-simmering rage about TIMEC's campaign of retaliatory racism, and my ongoing sadness at the puzzling irony of Dr. Polonsky's untimely murder. Then, in February of 2013, the tragic incidents of the news stories involving 34-year-old black Los Angeles Police Officer Christopher Dorner took prominence in the media news cycle.

As I sat stunned and in shock, I listened and watched the televised news reports of Dorner's violent outbursts of pent-up rage, purportedly over his having been summarily ostracized and dismissed from that police force, after his alleged dutiful reporting of an incident of bullying misconduct made against a member of the public, allegedly perpetrated by his own training officer. I felt a terrible, reflexive pain of rage remembrance twisting again, deep within my spirit, as the rampage of carnage continued to mount; I could not help but feel, that if my book had already been completely written, published and perhaps even read by that particular police officer, he could have made his way to understand that the feelings of being trapped in isolation, which he was clearly experiencing and going through, were not brand new, and were certainly not uniquely and individually formed and designed to destroy him, black United States Naval Reservist Chris Dorner, in particular.

In September of 2013, another black former United States Naval Reservist with mental health issues, 34 year-old Aaron Alexis, abruptly attacked and killed at least 12 people in a mass shooting which also wounded 14 others at a secure Naval Shipyard military facility in Washington, D.C., before eventually being shot and killed by responding officers.

Perhaps my written words might have been able, had they been available, to compel someone such as Christopher Dorner, or any other, violence prone individual sick and seething with rage today, to seek and find the help of professional psychological counseling, as I did with the late Dr. Ira Polonsky. Counseling which could possibly have helped them to please consider the understanding, and then, the eventual knowing, that while fighting white racism in the American workplace is an ongoing journey, it is actually, when broken down to its simplicity, only a legal matter, and in fact, a potentially winnable legal matter, and not a clarion call to bloody, violent war in the workplace.

In October of 2013, black Miami Dolphins offensive lineman Jonathan Martin left the team in midseason, reportedly after suffering from mental and emotional stress symptoms due to excessive bullying from white veteran teammate Richie Incognito. Many hardcore football fans have publicly derided Martin as being "too soft", for the brutal "reality" of their sport while, officially, the National Football

League (NFL) and the Dolphins organization have been thoroughly reviewing and investigating the matter. Perhaps the real reason that Martin's mental health situation has initially and seriously received prompt and actual, adequate review, as a legal corporate matter, is due to the fact that both of his parents are Harvard Law-educated attorneys.

In my opinion, white racist workplace bigots shall still continue to daily, and as a preferred personal issue of practice, persistently attempt to gradually strip away the protective outer shell of humanity from black people for their own insidious amusement. They even have a colloquial term which they use to describe what happens when a black person has been successfully pushed beyond the boiling point of rage, and then chooses to set all capacity to reason aside; they condescendingly call it "Chimping-Out".

To "chimp-out" is to publicly rage violently, and noisily, before physically exploding with chaos and destructive intent, until successfully being brought back, into a more socially appropriate and coherent, calm, form and order, "by the authorities", into a more moderate behavior (or, even sudden death) deemed properly acceptable in appearance and demeanor, and certainly one more adequately equipped to project mandatory White American-like assimilation.

I've personally decided, for myself, that I no longer have the luxury of wasting my time "sitting and silently sulking" alone and to myself, with my sad story about the brutal and racist viciousness of the TIMEC Corporation. I believe that this pertinent dialogue about the outrageous and dangerous foolishness of systematic racist oppression in the workplace must now officially begin, out in the open and for everyone to examine, so that in the future, perhaps a few very important lives of other people who are also truly loved and genuinely cared about, might actually be saved.

In Memory Of

Dr. Ira Eugene Polonsky, PhD. - Psychologist, January 9, 1941 - November 1, 2005

Christopher Jordan Dorner - United States Navy Reserve - Los Angeles Police Department,
June 4, 1979 - February 12, 2013

Alfredox Publishing Group

Alfredox Publishing Group is the group that designed the Book and worked with DanBump Publishing Group to get their first of many books published.

Feel free to contact Alfredox Publishing Group for Self-Publishing Assistance, Marketing and Promotions and all other aspects of getting your book to the masses at: alfredoxpublishing@yahoo.com.

28262057R00050

Made in the USA
Charleston, SC
05 April 2014